CULTURE SMART!

MEXICO

Russell Maddicks

·K·U·P·E·R·A·R·D·

This book is available for special discounts for bulk purchases
for sales promotions or premiums. Special editions, including
personalized covers, excerpts of existing books, and corporate
imprints, can be created in large quantities for special needs.

For more information contact Kuperard publishers
at the address below.

ISBN 978 1 85733 850 8
This book is also available as an e-book: eISBN 978 1 85733 851 5

British Library Cataloguing in Publication Data
A CIP catalogue entry for this book is available from the
British Library

First published in Great Britain
by Kuperard, an imprint of Bravo Ltd
59 Hutton Grove, London N12 8DS
Tel: +44 (0) 20 8446 2440   Fax: +44 (0) 20 8446 2441
www.culturesmart.co.uk
Inquiries: sales@kuperard.co.uk

Series Editor Geoffrey Chesler
Design Bobby Birchall

Printed in Malaysia

About the Author

RUSSELL MADDICKS is an award-winning, BBC-trained journalist, translator, and travel writer. A graduate in Economic and Social History from the University of Hull, England, he has spent the last twenty years traveling, living, and working in Latin America, most recently as a Regional Specialist for BBC Monitoring. He has visited Mexico on many extended trips, always finding some new and unusual facet to explore. He is also the author of *Culture Smart! Venezuela*, *Culture Smart! Ecuador* (which won the Gold Prize at the Pearl of the Pacific International Travel Journalism Awards at FITE in 2015), *Culture Smart! Cuba* (co-author), and the *Bradt Guide to Venezuela*.

The Culture Smart! series is continuing to expand.
For further information and latest titles visit
www.culturesmart.co.uk

The publishers would like to thank **CultureSmart!**Consulting for its help in researching and developing the concept for this series.

CultureSmart!Consulting creates tailor-made seminars and consultancy programs to meet a wide range of corporate, public-sector, and individual needs. Whether delivering courses on multicultural team building in the USA, preparing Chinese engineers for a posting in Europe, training call-center staff in India, or raising the awareness of police forces to the needs of diverse ethnic communities, it provides essential, practical, and powerful skills worldwide to an increasingly international workforce.

For details, visit www.culturesmartconsulting.com

CultureSmart!Consulting and **CultureSmart!** guides have both contributed to and featured regularly in the weekly travel program "Fast Track" on BBC World TV.

contents

contents

Map of Mexico

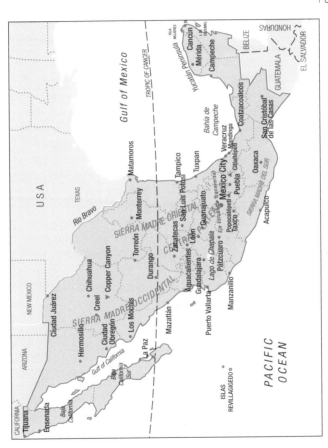

introduction

The third-largest country in Latin America, and home to 119 million people, Mexico is hugely diverse. It encompasses strong regional variations, major socioeconomic divisions, rural backwaters where time seems to have stopped, and chaotic urban centers like Mexico City, one of the most densely populated, maddening, and stimulating cities in the world.

Famed for its well-preserved archaeological sites, charming cobblestoned colonial towns, and beautiful beaches on both the Pacific and Atlantic coasts, Mexico is a major magnet for tourists. Whether they come to ride the Copper Canyon train in Chihuahua, watch whales in Baja California, or trek to jungle-covered Mayan temples in the deep south, visitors are increasing in number, despite negative news reports about drug dealers and spats with the US about migration. These problems, though real enough, should be seen in the wider context of a society going through great social and economic changes.

This complex and fascinating country, with its tumultuous history and rich cultural and culinary legacy, is the place where the European and pre-Columbian civilizations first clashed. The repercussions of the meeting in 1519 between the Spanish conquistador Hernán Cortés and the Aztec Emperor Montezuma II, and the subsequent devastation wrought by the Spanish Conquest, are still felt today, reflected in the Mexicans' attitudes toward race and national identity.

Culture Smart! Mexico takes you beyond the usual stereotypes of spicy food, Spaghetti-Western sombreros, and mariachi music into the heart of Mexican society. It describes the dynamics of daily life, the central importance of family, the annual cycle of Catholic feasts and fiestas, and how Mexicans socialize and meet members of the opposite sex. There is advice on how to negotiate a Mexican menu, on which delicious dishes you should try, on the differences between the local spirits tequila and mescal, and on tipping at the end of your meal. There is information on traveling safely and the best transport options for exploring the country. For business travelers there are sections on Mexico's economy, the general business culture, and tips on how to succeed in the local business environment.

We go behind the scenes to meet Mexico's masked *luchadores* (wrestlers), the authors, like Octavio Paz, Juan Rulfo, and Laura Esquivel, who have laid bare the Mexican soul, and the movie directors, like Alejandro González Iñárritu, Alfonso Cuarón, and Guillermo del Toro, who have helped to usher in a new golden age of Mexican cinema.

Mexican culture has remained so distinctive because of the pride that ordinary people feel in their pre-Hispanic past, their independence heroes, their unique musical traditions, and their tongue-tingling food, which is appreciated all over the world. *Culture Smart! Mexico* sets out to introduce you to the proud, spiritual, fiesta-loving, defiant, dynamic, fatalistic, fun-loving, food-obsessed, and hugely creative Mexican people and the extraordinary country they call home.

Key Facts

Official Name	Estados Unidos Mexicanos (United Mexican States)	Federal Republic of 31 states and Ciudad de México (CDMX)
Population	Approx. 120 million (2015 est.)	
Capital City	Ciudad de México	Pop. 9 million (capital); 22 million (metropolitan area)
Main Cities	Guadalajara (pop. 4.5 million), Monterrey (pop. 4.2 million), Puebla (pop. 2.3 million), Tijuana (pop. 1.8 million)	
Area	761,606 sq. miles (1,972,550 sq. km)	Third-largest country in Latin America
Geography	Bordered by the USA to the north, Guatemala and Belize to the south, with Atlantic and Pacific coasts.	Biologically diverse
Climate	Subtropical	Dry season December–April/May. Rainy season June–November. Average highs 81°F (27°C) in June; lows 70°F (21°C) in January
Ethnic Makeup	Mestizo (mixed race Spanish-Indigenous) 64%; Indigenous 14%; European descent 8%; Afro-Mexican 1.2%; Asian 1%; Arab 1%; US 1% (2015)	
Life Expectancy	75.4 years (men 72.6, women 78) (2015)	

Infant Mortality	11 deaths per 1,000 live births (2015)	
Language	Main language Spanish	68 indigenous languages
Literacy Rate	94.4% (2015, UNESCO)	
Religion	Roman Catholic 82%; Protestants, Evangelicals, Jehovah's Witnesses 8%. Small Jewish community	
Government	Federal Republic with President elected every six years	Two legislative chambers: Senate, Chamber of Deputies
Press	Hundreds of newspapers including *Reforma, La Jornada*; sensationalist tabloids	
Television	TV Azteca, Televisa produce popular *telenovelas* (soap operas). Cable, Satellite, Netflix available in main cities, tourist areas	
Currency	Mexican Peso ($), divided into 100 centavos	
GDP Per Capita	US $10,326 (2014, UN)	
Electricity	110 volts, 60 Hz	European appliances need 2-prong flat or round adaptors.
Internet Domain	.mx	
Video/DVD	NTSC–DVD Zone 4	
Telephone	Mexico's country code is 52.	City codes: Mexico City 55; Guadalajara 33; Monterrey 81; Mérida 999; Cancún 998
Time Zone	UTC/GMT -5 to -8 hours	Daylight Saving from April to October

LAND &
PEOPLE

chapter one

GEOGRAPHICAL SNAPSHOT

The smallest of the countries that make up North America and the third-largest Latin American country after Brazil and Argentina, Mexico covers an area of 761,610 square miles (1,972,550 sq. km)—roughly three times the size of the North American state of Texas, or eight times the size of the United Kingdom. It is bordered by the Gulf of California and the Pacific Ocean to the east and the Gulf of Mexico and the Caribbean to the west, and stretches from the US states of California, Arizona, New Mexico, and Texas in the north to the Central American countries of Guatemala in the south and Belize in the southeast.

The country's largest river is the Río Bravo (Rio Grande in the USA), which marks the border with Texas and flows into the Gulf of Mexico. The largest lake is Lago de Chapala, in Jalisco State, home to Mexico's largest US expat community.

The country sits on the Tropic of Cancer and the terrain is extremely diverse, with large expanses of arid scrubland in the northern Sonoran and Chihuahuan Deserts, temperate highlands running down the center of the country, swamps and seasonally flooded plains on the Gulf Coast, underground rivers and cenote wells in the Yucatán Peninsula, and lush rainforest in the southern state of Chiapas.

The central Mexican plateau is home to Mexico City, one of the biggest metropolitan areas in the world with an estimated population of 22 million people. The central highlands are flanked by two impressive mountain ranges—the Sierra Madre Oriental in the east and the Sierra Madre Occidental in the west, which is famous for the jagged valleys of Copper Canyon, Mexico's answer to the Grand Canyon.

In the south, the Eje Volcánico Transversal (Trans-Mexican Volcanic Belt) is named for its snow-covered

volcanic peaks. The smouldering cone of Popocatépetl
is Mexico's second highest mountain at 17,802 feet
(5,426 m) and can be clearly seen on smog-free days
from Mexico City, some forty-three miles (70 km) to
the northwest. The country's most active volcano, it
has erupted several times in the last few years.

An Aztec legend that mirrors Shakespeare's tragedy
Romeo and Juliet states that the nearby volcano of
Iztaccíhuatl (Nahuatl for "white woman") was a young
maiden who fell in love with the warrior Popocatépetl
and took her own life when she was falsely told he
had perished in battle. The four volcanic cones of
Iztaccíhuatl rise to 17,160 feet (5,230 m) and locals say
they mark out the silhouette of a sleeping woman. The
furious eruptions of Popocatépetl, they explain, are
the rage of the brave warrior who lost his only love.

Citlaltépetl, or Pico de Orizaba—a dormant
volcano—is the highest mountain in Mexico at
18,490 feet (5,636 m) and the third-highest in North
America after Denali (Mount McKinley) in the USA
and Mount Logan in Canada.

The Trans-Mexican Volcanic Belt is also home
to Mexico's rare and endangered oyamel (sacred fir)

forests. From October to March these high-peak forests pay host to hundreds of millions of monarch butterflies (*Danaus plexippus*), which come here on a 2,500-mile migration from Canada to overwinter. Considered one of nature's great spectacles, the monarch migration attracts a large number of naturalists and tourists each year and the oyamel forests in Michoacan State are now protected within the Reserva de la Biosfera Mariposa Monarca (Monarch Butterfly Biosphere Reserve).

Mexico has the most biosphere reserves in Latin America, with forty-one of its unique and fragile ecosystems protected by UNESCO. El Vizcaino in central Baja California is Mexico's largest protected area, covering the whale-calving areas of Ojo de Liebre, Laguna San Ignacio, and parts of the Gulf of California. This is the best place in the world to watch whales and other marine life. The famous submariner Jacques Cousteau called the Gulf of California "the world's aquarium." Thousands of tourists come each year to see gray whales, blue whales, sperm whales, whale sharks, and dolphins during the whale-watching season from mid-December to mid-April.

Down in Quintana Roo State, in the southern Yucatán, the Sian Ka'an Biosphere Reserve is a UNESCO World Heritage Site that covers mangroves, tropical forest, and offshore access to the Mesoamerican Reef, home to a richer diversity of marine life than Australia's famed Great Barrier Reef.

CLIMATE

Temperatures in Mexico can vary considerably, depending on location and elevation, with hot, dry deserts in the north, snow and ice in high mountain valleys, cool climes in the high central plateau, hot and humid rainforest in Chiapas, hot and sticky swamplands on the Gulf Coast, and a warm year-round climate on the coast.

The main seasons are the *temporada seca* (dry season) from December to April, which is also known as *invierno* (winter), and the *temporada de lluvias* (rainy season) from May to November, which is also known as *verano* (summer). The hottest months are May and June, and the wettest months coincide with the hurricane season from late June to November.

Temperatures in Mexico City vary a few degrees from warm daytime highs of 71.6°F (22°C) in December to 80.6°F (27°C) in June, and night-time lows of 42.8°F (6°C) in December and 53.6°F (12°C) in June.

PEOPLE

Mexico is often described as a *mestizo* nation, from the Spanish word *mestizaje,* meaning "mixed ancestry." Some 64 percent of the population are identified as *mestizo* by researchers, but the country's racial reality is much more nuanced than the statistics suggest, and most people prefer to identify themselves simply as

Mexicans. The sixty-two Amerindian indigenous groups recognized by the state make up about 14 percent of the population, for example, but 21 percent of those surveyed for the 2015 census self-identified as indigenous. There are nearly 2 million speakers of Nahuatl, the language of the ancient Aztecs, nearly a million speakers of Yucatec Maya, half a million Zapotec speakers, and the same number of Mixtec speakers.

The recent inclusion of Afro-Mexicans in the census acknowledges for the first time the descendants of Mexico's African slaves, who make up about 1.2 percent of the population, with important communities in Costa Chica, on the coast of Oaxaca, and in towns like Mandinga and Mozambique, near Veracruz.

Mexicans still refer to Arabic people—both Christian and Muslim—as "Turcos" (Turks), a legacy of the period before and after the First World War when many Lebanese Christians came to Mexico from a collapsing Ottoman Empire. Although small in number (some 400,000), the Lebanese are strongly represented in business and the professions. Famous Lebanese Mexicans include the multibillionaire Carlos Slim, one of the world's richest men, and the Hollywood actress and producer Salma Hayek.

Chinese communities were established in the nineteenth century. There is a large Barrio Chino (Chinatown) in Mexico City. Another, La Chinesca, in Mexicali, boasts the highest concentration of Cantonese-style restaurants in Mexico.

Blue-eyed, blond-haired German and Dutch Mennonites have established small but culturally distinct farming communities in the states of Aguascalientes, Chihuahua, Durango, and Zacatecas. The largest Mennonite group in Latin America is to be found in Ciudad Cuauhtémoc in Chihuahua.

THE STATES OF MEXICO

Mexico is a Federal Republic with thirty-one states and, until recently, a Distrito Federal (Federal District) representing the capital city and seat of government. In 2018, the Distrito Federal, better known by its acronym DF (day-efay), will be officially replaced by Ciudad de México (Mexico City), giving it more of the autonomous powers granted to states. The rebranding process has already started with the city's new abbreviation CDMX widely displayed on hoardings. Taxis are also being repainted pink and white to match the city's new colors. Traditionally referred to as "Chilangos" or "Defeños" (residents of DF), or irreverently as "Defectuosos" (defects), the inhabitants of the capital will also have a new name: "Mexiqueños." This should not be confused with "Mexiquenses" (people from Mexico State) or "Mexicanos."

A BRIEF HISTORY

The epic, turbulent, and remarkable story of Mexico covers such a vast swathe of time that it is only possible to give a brief sketch of the arrival of the first nomadic mammoth-hunters; the rise and fall of the great civilizations of the pre-Columbian era; the conquest of the Aztecs by the Spanish; the fight for independence; foreign military interventions; the loss of territory to the USA; the Revolution; and the building of a modern democracy. For an instant snapshot of Mexico's colorful history there is no better place to start than Diego Rivera's magnificent mural that graces the staircase of the National Palace in Mexico City.

The First Americans

The traditional theory of the peopling of the Americas suggests that bands of hunter-gatherers came across the Bering Strait from Siberia in the last ice age, some 12,000 years ago. However, new dates of stone tools from Florida suggest humans were in the Americas by at least 14,500 years ago, and some archaeologists have suggested dates as far back as 45,000 years ago. The most complete skeleton of an early American so far discovered is a teenage girl that scientists have named Naia. Her well-preserved skull and skeleton date back 12–13,000 years and were found—alongside bones of pleistocene mammals such as saber-tooth cats, giant ground sloths, and cave bears—in an underwater cave system called Hoyo Negro (Black Hole) in the Yucatán Peninsula. Early Americans, also known as Paleo-Indians, hunted giant mammals, such as Columbian mammoths, until these became extinct around 9,000 years ago, through overhunting or climate change. The bones of some fifty mammoths have been excavated around Mexico City.

Following the domestication of corn (*Zea mays*) from a plant called *teosinte* about 10,000 years ago, several important civilizations arose in Mesoamerica (Middle America), a cultural area that extends from central Mexico to Nicaragua and Costa Rica in Central America.

Formative Period

The first major group to emerge in Mesoamerica are the Olmec, who between 1,800 and 400 BCE settled in cities or ceremonial centers in San Lorenzo, La Venta, Laguna de los Cerros, and Tres Zapotes on the Gulf Coast. They built earth pyramids to worship their gods, carved large, enigmatic stone heads of their warrior kings, practiced cranial modification to distinguish castes, traded with distant groups in Central America for jadeite and serpentine, and had a religion that incorporated strange "were-jaguars" (half human and half feline). Sometimes described as the Mother Culture of Mesoamerica, the Olmec are also believed to have used a complex calendar based on astronomical observations and to have made blood sacrifices to their gods. Although some glyphic inscriptions survive, there is not enough early Olmec writing to give any deep insights into their beliefs or social structures. Even their name has come to us from the later Aztecs, who called a contemporary people on the Gulf Coast Olmeca (the rubber people). A 3,000-year-old rubber ball excavated at the Olmec site of El Manati, in Veracruz, is evidence that the Olmec played the Mesoamerican ball game, a ceremonial face-off between two teams that had a ritual significance.

Pre-Classic and Classic Period
From about 150 BCE to 150 CE, at the end of the Pre-Classic period, important city-states arose, such as the Zapotec city of Monte Alban in modern-day Oaxaca and Teotihuacán in the Valley of Mexico. The Classic Period from 250 to 900 CE saw the Maya civilization reach its zenith across modern-day Mexico, Guatemala, and Honduras in city-states run by warrior chieftains such as Palenque, Uxmal, and Chichén Itzá.

Teotihuacán
At its height this imposing city of stone pyramids and ceremonial plazas was home to some 200,000 people, but because there are no hieroglyphic inscriptions

to fill in the details we know little about those who ruled here. The name comes from the Aztecs who visited it hundreds of years after it had been burned and abandoned. They were so impressed by the monumental scale of the architecture that they called it Teotihuacán, Nahuatl for "Birthplace of the Gods." The Pyramid of the Sun is the biggest pyramid structure in the Americas, and a tunnel found under the Pyramid of Quetzalcoatl (the Plumed Serpent) is shedding new light on the religious ceremonies practiced there.

The Maya
Like the city-states of Ancient Greece, the Mayan population centers that flourished in Southern Mexico, Honduras, and Guatemala shared a common culture, including a huge pantheon of gods, a complex calendar based on astronomical observations, an advanced mathematical system employing zero, and a sophisticated hieroglyphic writing system. Warrior kings ruled these city-states, and their stone monuments list royal dynasties, wars of conquest, and human sacrifice. Brightly colored murals in the Mayan city of Bonampak, in Chiapas, show ritual bloodletting

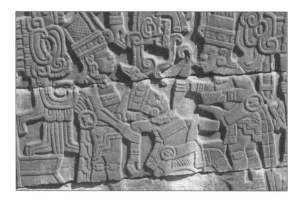

and the sacrifice of captive lords. Dating to 790 CE, they mark the beginning of the end, as climate change, poor harvests, and unsustainable populations caused the main Mayan city-states to collapse.

The Post-Classic Period

One group that established itself at present-day Tula was the militaristic Toltecs, whose pyramids feature standing warriors carrying *atlatls* (spear throwers) and who established a trading empire from about 800 to 1000 CE. As yet unexplained by archaeologists, Toltec influence also appears 800 miles away in the Post-Classic architecture of the Mayan city of Chichén Itzá, including stone statues of seated warriors, called chacmools, and a central temple, El Castillo, dedicated to Kukulkan, the feathered serpent that the Toltecs worshipped as Quetzalcoatl. This Toltec style of building coincides with the brief resurgence of Chichén Itzá and other Mayan cities around 900 CE.

The period also saw the arrival in central Mexico of nomadic Chichimec tribes from the northern deserts. One of those tribes, the Aztecs, would go on to build the most powerful empire ever seen in Mesoamerica.

The Aztecs

Following a prophecy from Huitzilopochtli, god of the sun, fire, and human sacrifice, the Mexica tribe left their ancestral homeland in Aztlán and wandered for many years until they came across an island in Lake Texcoco and found the sign they had been seeking: an eagle perched on a cactus devouring a snake. On that spot, in 1325, they built the city of Tenochtitlán. That's the legend, at least, and the image of the eagle is enshrined in Mexico's flag.

The real story of the Mexica is of a vassal tribe to more powerful neighbors, who, over a century of fighting for others, grew powerful enough to take control of the city-states around Lake Texcoco and build their own empire. At its height, just before the Sanish conquest, this vast trading empire extended down to Nicaragua and Costa Rica. The basis of Aztec religion was sacrifice, either by ritual bloodletting or by full-on human heart extraction, because they believed that the gods of the sun, Huitzilopochtli, and rain, Tlaloc, had to be nourished with blood. War became a ritual enterprise, and death, blood, and sacrifice were exalted in elegant Aztec poems. Warriors dressed as eagles and jaguars fought so-called "flowery wars" with neighboring states where the object was not to kill enemies on the battlefield but to bring back captives whose hearts would be cut out at the top of the Templo Mayor, the vast stone pyramid at the heart of Tenochtitlán.

It is easy to focus on the bloodletting that left the steps of the great pyramid sticky with gore, but the

Aztec city was also a marvel of organization, home to 200,000 citizens, who were fed by an ingenious system of floating gardens called *chinampas* that can still be appreciated in the Mexico City suburb of Xochimilco.

The hierarchy of the Aztec Empire started at the top with the emperor and the royal family. Then came the priests and the warrior generals. The *pochteca* (traders) formed a middle class, then there were craftsmen and the rest of the population, who received food and goods for working in agriculture and construction. There was no money economy: trade was carried out through barter, and goods came to Tenochtitlán as tribute from conquered states, who were able to keep their own leaders.

The Spanish Conquest

The conquest of the mighty Aztec Empire by a group of six hundred Spanish conquistadors is one of the key events in world history: a collision of the Old World with a New World in which the Europeans were victorious and an advanced American civilization was stopped in its tracks. Like the conquest of the Incas in Peru, the conquest of the Aztecs hinges to some extent on the more efficient arms of the Spanish, who brought steel, horses, and cannons to the battlefield. But it was aided by the Old World diseases of smallpox and influenza that swept before the invaders, decimating local populations and sapping their ability to defend themselves. The Spanish policy of seizing the emperor was crucial at the beginning of both campaigns. In the long run it was the key alliances with disaffected tribes, providing thousands more fighters, that allowed a small band of soldiers to conquer a vast territory, although the full conquest of present-day Mexico took 150 years to complete.

Cortés and Moctezuma

In February 1519, the Spanish conquistador Hernán Cortés left the Spanish-controlled island of Cuba to explore the coast of Mexico. His first stop was the island of Cozumel, where he found a Spanish sailor, Jerónimo de Aguilar, who had been shipwrecked and had spent eight years with the local Maya. In April the Spanish defeated an indigenous army near the Grijalva River, and Cortés was presented with a girl, called Malinalli or Malintzin, who could speak both Maya and Nahuatl, the language of the Aztecs. La Malinche, as she is known, played a key role in the conquest and had a son by Cortés, but has been vilified by later Mexican writers and historians for betraying her people and aiding the invaders.

When the Spanish arrived in modern-day Veracruz on the Gulf Coast, news of the curious strangers reached the ears of the Aztec emperor, Moctezuma II, who sent ambassadors inviting them to Tenochtitlán. The journey took three months, but by the time Cortés arrived he had fought many battles and made new alliances with local tribes.

After meeting Moctezuma, Cortés immediately took him prisoner, demanding a huge ransom for his release. Cortés then defeated a military expedition sent by the governor of Cuba, who wanted the spoils of this new land for himself.

After an Aztec revolt broke out, led by Moctezuma's younger brother Cuitláhuac, Moctezuma was killed, either by the Spanish or his own people. On June 30, 1520, "La Noche Triste" (the Night of Sorrows), as the Spaniards called it, the embattled Spanish were forced to flee the city, resulting in many of Cortes' men being killed, or sacrificed by the Aztec priests. It was the first major defeat for the Spaniards, but it came too late to save the Aztecs. On May 26, 1521, the Spanish returned with thousands of native warriors and cut off all the causeways joining the island city of Tenochtitlán to the mainland. The new emperor Cuauhtémoc put up brave resistance to a nearly three-month seige but the

Aztecs were finally brought to surrender by famine and disease and on August 13, 1521, the city fell. Cuauhtémoc was executed.

On the ruins of the Aztec capital the Spanish built Mexico City and began the conquest of the rest of the country. Wars were fought with the Chichimecs and other tribes, and new towns were founded to exploit rich seams of silver. Only the remote Maya communities who fiercely defended their southern forests were able to survive into colonial times, but eventually even they fell. Before the arrival of Cortés an estimated 25 million Amerindians lived in the area we now know as Mexico. Within a few years, armed conquest and disease had reduced that number to a few million survivors.

The Colonial Era

The colonization of Mexico followed the pattern employed by the Spanish across the Americas. As early as 1531 a shrine was built to the Virgin of Guadalupe on the site of a temple to the Aztec Earth Mother Tonantzin. The huge cathedral that dominates the Zócalo in Mexico City was built with stone from the Templo Mayor, the toppled Aztec pyramid of Tenochtitlán—the ruins of which you can visit today, thanks to a major archaeological project. All across the country this pattern was repeated: Catholic churches were erected on top of "heathen" temples, idols were smashed, and thousands of hieroglyphic bark books were burned by overzealous priests eager to convert their new flocks.

Hundreds of towns were built on the Spanish model, *haciendas* brought in horses and livestock, the indigenous population was put to work on the land or in silver mines, and Catholic missionaries carried the conversion of the indigenous population to the wilder frontiers of what was now the Virreinato de Nueva España (Vice-Royalty of New Spain). The viceroy represented the Spanish monarch and all productive labor in the colony had one goal: the enrichment of the Spanish Crown. Trade with other countries was prohibited, even trade between neighboring Vice-Royalties. The idea was that all goods would be imported from Spain and all raw materials exported to Spain.

A colonial class structure began to develop and people were categorized into *castas,* with Spaniards from Spain at the top, and *criollos* (Spaniards born in the Americas) below them. *Mestizos,* people of indigenous and Spanish descent, were in the middle, Amerindians came next, and Africans brought over as slaves were at the bottom.

The Cry of Independence

At the turn of the nineteenth century strict colonial restrictions on trade and commerce had become an onerous burden for the conservative *criollo* elite, and higher taxes were imposed from Spain. The USA had revolted against British colonial rule and won its independence in 1776, and the ideas of the French Revolution circulated among more radical thinkers who longed for greater freedom. The spark came when the French emperor Napoleon Bonaparte invaded and occupied the Iberian peninsula in 1808, deposing the Spanish monarch, King Ferdinand VII.

The first cry of independence came on September 16, 1810, when at 5:00 a.m. Father Miguel Hidalgo rang the bells of his small parish church in Dolores, near Guanajuato, and called on Mexican patriots to take up arms and fight for their freedom. The words he uttered are lost to time. but were along the lines of "*Mexicanos! Viva México!*" and a reference to ending bad government by the *gachupines*, a term used for the Spanish. Alongside Ignacio Allende, he raised an army of 100,000 sympathizers and led them with a flag depicting the Virgin of Guadalupe, promising an end to taxes on indigenous peasants and the abolition of slavery. After taking several towns and cities and threatening Mexico City itself, Hidalgo was captured and executed by firing squad on July 30, 1811.

In 1813 the banner of independence was taken up by José María Morelos, whose uprising was crushed in 1815. Eventually it was the Criollos who achieved independence under the conservative Agustín de Iturbide, who took Mexico City on September 27, 1821, and then reigned as Emperor Agustín I for nearly two years before being deposed and sent into exile.

On November 1, 1823, the Federal Republic of the United Mexican States was declared and enshrined in the constitution of 1824. Iturbide returned from exile in 1824 only to be arrested and sentenced to execution by firing squad. His last words were: "I die merrily, because I die among you. I die with honor, not as a traitor."
Now considered one of the great heroes of Mexico, Iturbide designed the national flag.

Upheaval and War With the USA

The new nation was thrown into chaos as free-trade, secular liberals fought for power with conservatives tied to the Catholic Church. There were some thirty presidents in the fifty years following independence, and General Antonio López de Santa Anna was president on eleven occasions. This period saw Mexico lose over half its territory to the USA. Texas went first, seceding in 1836. (Remember the Alamo?) Then, in 1846, US President James K. Polk ordered the invasion of Mexico, leading to the fall of Mexico City to US troops, and the signing of the Treaty of Guadalupe Hidalgo in 1848, which ceded New Mexico, Nevada, Utah, Arizona, Colorado, and California to the USA.

La Reforma

The humiliating defeat and loss of territory to the USA led to the exile of Santa Anna in 1854 and an attempt at reform led by Benito Juárez, a Zapotec Indian and liberal lawyer, who drafted the Constitution of 1857, enshrining the separation of Church and state and granting land rights to indigenous peasants.

A conservative backlash led to the War of the Reform, which again threw the country into turmoil, culminating in a bizarre plan hatched by conservatives in Mexico and Napoleon III to install Maximilian of Habsburg on a Mexican throne.

A Mexican Emperor

Maximilian arrived backed by French troops and declared himself Maximilian I of Mexico on April 10, 1864. A liberal at heart, he soon lost the support of his conservative backers and faced a guerrilla war from the outset from fervent followers of Benito Juárez. When the backing of Napoleon III waned in 1866 the game was up for the unwanted emperor, who was captured in Querétaro and shot by a firing squad on June 19, 1867.

Porfiriato leads to Revolution

General Porfirio Díaz, who had fought against the French, took power in 1876 and didn't let go until he was forced into exile in 1911. Elected president seven times in a mockery of democracy, he did achieve a peace and stability in the country that allowed business, especially foreign businesses, to thrive. However, rural peasants forced off their lands by large landowners, and harsh industrial conditions in the cities sowed the seeds for the Mexican Revolution.

Revolution and Chaos

A liberal landowner, Francisco I. Madero was an unlikely revolutionary, but after the presidential election was stolen from him by Porfirio Díaz he made an impassioned call to arms from exile in Texas on November 20, 1910. The simmering resentment of Mexico's oppressed peasants and workers had come to the boil and charismatic leaders emerged like Francisco "Pancho" Villa, a former bandit from Chihuahua, and Emiliano Zapata from Morelos, who called for "*Tierra y Libertad*" (Land and Freedom). Madero became president, but the Revolution continued as faction fought faction and the country descended into anarchy. Estimates put the death toll in the ten years of the Mexican Revolution at a million people; some scholars believe it was higher. Madero was assassinated in 1913, Emiliano Zapata in 1919, and Pancho Villa in 1923.

Modern Mexico Emerges

The Constitution of February 5, 1917, marked the end of the Revolution, but it would take many years for full peace to be achieved. The short-lived Cristero War, an anti-Catholic drive by President Plutarco Elías Calles, was bloody and divisive but delivered a secular state. One of the most important events at this time was the 1929 founding of the Partido Nacional Revolucionario (National Revolutionary Party), which later became the Partido Revolucionario Institutional (PRI) and controlled the Mexican presidency for seventy-one years.

Mexico flourished both economically and artistically under President Lázaro Cárdenas, who delivered on land and labor reforms and nationalized the oil industry in 1938. Muralists like Diego Rivera, David Alfaro Siqueiros, and José Clemente Orozco helped to shape this new Mexican pride, rooted in an indigenous past and revolutionary struggle.

Stability and Growth

From the 1940s to the 1960s booming oil wealth and an emerging manufacturing industry based in Mexico City, Monterrey, and along the US border helped to fund public works and ambitious housing projects. Throughout this process, political stability was provided by the de-facto one-party state run by the monolithic PRI, which Peruvian novelist Mario Vargas Llosa dubbed the "the perfect dictatorship." Rapid urbanization also saw shanty towns appear as people moved to the big cities in search of work.

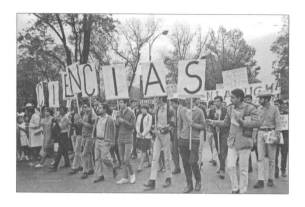

The Tlatelolco Massacre

In 1968, students inspired by the May riots in Paris took to the streets to air their grievances against the PRI government of Gustavo Díaz Ordaz. With the opening of the Olympic Games in Mexico City imminent, the government led a harsh crackdown to clear the streets of protesters. On October 2, unarmed students protesting at the Three Cultures Square in the Tlatelolco housing complex were attacked by soldiers with fixed bayonets backed up by tanks. Some estimates put the number of people killed as high as 3,000, sparking international outrage, but the Tlatelolco Massacre, as it came to be called, was never properly investigated under the PRI; even today the truth has yet to emerge.

NAFTA, the Zapatistas, and the PRI

When Carlos Salinas de Gortari became president in 1988 he embarked on a massive privatization program to stimulate the economy, stopping short of opening up the oil industry. The culmination of this economic overhaul came in 1994, when Mexico signed up to the North American Free Trade

Agreement (NAFTA), essentially opening its market to goods from the USA and Canada. The result was initially catastrophic for Mexican farmers, prompting a spike in Mexican migrants seeking work in the US, both legally and illegally, and increased tension in rural areas.

In rural Chiapas, the poorest state in Mexico, the reaction to NAFTA was an armed uprising by the Zapatista Army of National Liberation (ELZN), a group of intellectual radicals and indigenous peasant farmers inspired by the ideals of Emiliano Zapata. On New Year's Day 1994 the group seized control of San Cristóbal de las Casas, sparking immediate interest from news organizations in their mysterious leader, Subcomandante Marcos, who wore a balaclava to conceal his identity (much like a *lucha libre* superhero), and smoked a pipe like a university academic. International sympathy for the Zapatistas and the intense media spotlight probably stopped the army from more brutal repression, but the situation ended in an uneasy ceasefire negotiated in 1995 that has left the Zapatistas unmolested in their autonomous communities but with few of their demands met.

The effects of NAFTA have also impacted the PRI. In 2000 the PRI's seven-decade hold on power was finally broken with the election of President Vicente Fox of the Partido Acción Nacional (PAN). The pattern continued in 2006 with the election of

President Felipe Calderón, also from PAN, who made a game-changing decision to declare war on Mexico's drug cartels, resulting in a huge spike in cartel-related violence and deaths as the drug gangs militarized their own operations with high-caliber weapons. Some estimates put the death toll in Mexico's war on drugs during the period from 2006 to 2012 as high as 50–60,000.

The election of Enrique Peña Nieto in 2012 marked the return of a PRI president, but little has changed in the strategy to tackle the growing violence of the cartels. Reminiscent of the Tlatelolco Massacre, the involvement of local authorities in the disappearance and probable massacre of forty-three students on the night of September 26, 2014, in Iguala, has prompted protests across the country and calls for an end to corruption and impunity.

The ability of Sinaloa Cartel boss Joaquín "Chapo" Guzman to escape from high security prisons on two occasions—and be interviewed by Hollywood actor Sean Penn while on the run—has also been a source of embarrassment to the government.

GOVERNMENT

Mexico is a Federal Republic with thirty-one states and Ciudad de México (Mexico City), a new Federal entity representing the seat of government that replaces the Distrito Federal (DF). Voting in elections is mandatory and there is universal suffrage for all Mexicans over the age of eighteen.

The division of powers in Mexico is similar to the US system. The legislative branch is divided into a Senate, with 128 senators elected every six years, and a Chamber of Deputies, with 500 members elected every three years.

NATIONAL SYMBOLS

A source of great pride is the national flag, a vertical tricolor of green, white, and red, in use since the nineteenth-century wars of independence. The national coat of arms that appears in the center of the flag invokes the Aztec legend of the founding of Tenochtitlán and shows an eagle, with a snake held in one of its talons, perched on a prickly pear cactus growing from a rock in a lake.

National anthem: "Mexicanos, al Grito de Guerra" ("Mexicans, at the Cry of War") by Francisco González Bocanegra, music by Jaime Nunó.

National bird: *Quebrantahuesos Mexicano* (Northern Crested Caracara, *Caracara cheriway*).

National flower: Dahlia (*Dahlia pinnata*).

National tree: *Ahuehuete* (Montezuma Cypress, *Taxodium mucronatum*).

The executive branch is led by the president, who is the head of state and government and the Supreme Commander of the armed forces. The president can appoint a cabinet, the attorney general, military chiefs, and Supreme Court Justices.

Elections for president are held every six years and presidents can serve only one term. This restriction on reelection, known as the *sexenio,* was introduced to avoid a repetition of the "Santa Anna Age," when the Mexican general Antonio López de Santa Anna dominated politics and was president eleven times over a forty-year period, and the twenty-six years of the "Porfiriato," when Porfirio Díaz ruled the country.

The *sexenio* had little effect, however, in stopping the Partido Revolucionario Institucional (PRI) from running Mexico like a one-party state for seventy-one years (1929–2000), as outgoing presidents would simply name their successor.

State governors are also elected, serving a single six-year term, and state assemblies have the power to levy local taxes.

The states have their own courts with the power to rule on local cases, but appeals can be taken to the Supreme Court, the highest court in the land.

THE ECONOMY

Before joining the North American Free Trade Agreement (NAFTA) with the US and Canada in 1994 Mexico was dependent on oil for some 80 percent of its foreign currency earnings. Oil now represents only about 20 percent of total earnings due to diversification of the economy and the rapid growth of manufacturing industry, especially the large-scale assembly plants, or *maquiladoras*, along the border with the USA.

The opening up of the oil industry to foreign investment in 2013, a reform brought in by President Enrique Peña Nieto, aimed to increase oil exploration and investment in refining, but it will only have a major impact when oil prices begin to rise.

Apart from automobiles and domestic goods, Mexico has developed an important electronics industry and is expanding into aerospace. While the country has signed free trade agreements with forty-six countries, 80 percent of exports go to the USA. Raw materials and agricultural goods play a lesser role in the economy than they did pre-NAFTA, but Mexico continues to be the world's top producer of silver, avocados, and limes.

Meanwhile, an increasingly diverse and sophisticated service sector catering to Mexico's growing middle class is attracting ever greater foreign investment, especially in financial services.

On the downside, Mexico has not tackled the large income disparities between the rich and the poor, who make up some 33 percent of the population. Social, economic, and educational inequality also continue to blight the lives of those living in rural areas, and little has been done done to address the problems highlighted by the Zapatista uprising in 1994.

The lack of opportunities in the countryside produces a steady stream of economic migrants seeking work and a better life across the border. Remittances from Mexicans working in the USA have increased, and, although the exact figures are hard to nail down, in 2015 they were estimated at some US $24.8 billion, even higher than the amount earned from oil.

Despite the negative effects of the narco news stories pumped out by the international media, tourism continues to be a significant generator of income and jobs. Mexico is one of the top ten most popular tourist destinations in the world, according to the United Nations World Tourism Organization. Attractions like the Mayan pyramids of Yucatán, the world-class museums of Mexico City, the white-sand beaches of Cancun, and the magnificent whale watching in the lagoons and bays of Baja California, all help to attract a steadily rising number of tourists. In 2015, Mexico received over 32 million tourists, more than Russia and a similar number to the UK.

The majority of visitors come from the USA, either as tourists or to start a new life among the million or so US expatriates. Another driver of the economy, US expats are drawn by the proximity of Mexico to family and friends back home, the cheaper cost of living, and the country's strong cultural heritage, ancient and colonial cities, attractive handicrafts, and amazing food.

chapter two

VALUES & ATTITUDES

It is difficult to generalize about Mexicans, given that Mexico is such a large country encompassing so many distinct regions, each with its own culture, food, music, and customs. The country is further divided along socioeconomic lines by the huge disparities between the rich cosmopolitan elite, who educate their children in private schools and live behind high walls; the growing middle class, who aspire to more; and the many Mexicans left at the bottom of the pile, who struggle from day to day to make ends meet. Only a short period of travel in the country, or a visit to one of the many indigenous groups that live very distinct lives from the mainstream, is enough to conclude that there is not one Mexico but many.

RELIGION

The Roman Catholic religion has done much to shape beliefs and attitudes in Mexico since it was imposed on the population in the sixteenth century, and its influence continues to be strong. Over 80 percent of Mexicans identify as Catholics, religious festivities dominate the calendar, and life for the majority follows a cycle of baptisms, first communions, weddings, and funerals. One reason for the success of Catholicism is due to the pragmatism of the Jesuit and Franciscan monks who led the conversions and allowed indigenous Mexicans to incorporate their traditional beliefs into their new form of worship. This is most apparent in the folk festivals held on Catholic feast days that contain pre-Columbian elements, and in the joyous and playful nature of Mexico's Day of the Dead rituals that make them unique in the Catholic world.

FAMILY VALUES

Generally built around a strong mother figure, the family is hugely important to Mexicans. Few families are as large as they used to be, when a couple had seven or eight children, but the tradition of the extended family persists, with several generations often living under one roof, or close to each other. Old people are respected and are generally looked after by their families rather than going into residential homes to see out their last days.

Children are doted on and involved in social gatherings from an early age. Children's birthday parties will involve several generations of the family and take place at home, or in a park with a barbecue or picnic, and the obligatory *piñata* full of sweets, but they are first and foremost family events, to be enjoyed as much by the adults as the kids. Mexican children grow up to be confident, if a little spoiled, and tend not to have the teenage meltdown considered normal in the US and many parts of Europe that leaves them unable to communicate or have fun with anybody but other teenagers.

The concept of young people leaving the family home at eighteen to study or live alone as they do in the US or UK is still alien to most Mexicans, and they generally stay at home until they marry or have to migrate for work. This is partly for reasons of economy, but also because life is easier in an extended family as long as everybody gets on, especially for young men, who are rarely expected to cook or clean, are not often asked to contribute financially, and have plenty of time to socialize with friends. Even for those who have to migrate for work there is a round of birthdays, baptisms, weddings, and public holidays to keep cousins in contact and maintain family ties.

Poverty, or the absence of a father who might have several children with different partners, can cause families to break up, and it is not unusual for children to be raised by grandparents or aunts, or even relatives living far away in the US. But people will try to find a solution within the family before going to outside agencies.

Where women with young children have to work, it is typical for the grandparents to take over child minding, although well-off Mexicans may employ nannies and send their children to nurseries. The poorest single mothers are often forced to take their babies with them to informal jobs; you see them, with their babies strapped to their backs, selling food from street stalls or hawking newspapers, candies, and snacks on the streets or on buses. For some children, poverty and family breakup can lead to a dangerous life on the streets, but the Mexican authorities have done much in recent years to provide solutions for street kids.

Historic Fatalism

Young Mexicans may not recognize themselves in this portrayal, but if there is one characteristic that stands out from historical descriptions of the Mexican people it is a melancholic fatalism: a resignation that the worst will probably happen, that some inevitable doom is just around the corner, and that life is hard and pleasure fleeting. Historian Salvador de Madariaga argued that this fatalistic outlook is rooted in Mexico's violent past and the Spanish Conquest of the Aztecs, writing: "Every day, within the soul of every Mexican, Moctezuma dies and Cuauhtémoc is hanged."

PRIDE, HONOR, AND *MACHISMO*

Machismo is not unique to Mexico. Most Latin American countries have a macho stereotype to which many men still aspire: a strong, decisive, and stoic individual who is unafraid of danger and quick to defend any slight against his family or country, no matter the odds.

Tequila Tears

Lilting laments to lost love, Mexico's sad mariachi songs are sure-fire tear-jerkers – the musical equivalent of chopping onions for its macho men. The image of a despondent drinker dripping salty tears into his shot glass as he slumps on the bar of a *cantina* is immortalized in the song "Ella" (She) by Jose Alfredo Jimenez: "*Quise hallar el olvido al estilo Jalisco, pero aquellos mariachis y aquel tequila me hicieron llorar*" ("I wanted to forget in the style of Jalisco, but those mariachis and tequila made me cry").

Mariachi songs also reinforce the stereotype of the Mexican macho as a defiant loner who makes his own rules and answers to nobody. The attitude is summed up in another Jimenez classic "El Rey" (The King): "*Con dinero y sin dinero hago siempre lo que quiero y mi palabra es la ley. No tengo trono ni reina, ni nadie quien me comprenda, pero sigo siendo el rey.*" ("With money or without money I always do what I want and my word is the law. I have no throne or queen, or anybody who understands me, but I am still the king.")

On the positive side, old-school macho men are expected to be generous and show respect to women, especially mothers and grandmothers. On the downside, they can be aggressive and demanding, and can take rejection badly.

Piropos (romantic compliments) are a throwback to the days when men would write love poetry to their *amores*. Mexican men are still romantic (just listen to the love songs in the Mexican charts); but overly sexual *piropos*—like wolf whistles—come across as crude and closer to harassment. Casual sexism is everywhere, from the home, where boys are allowed to play while girls are expected to help in the kitchen, to the workplace, where women are expected to dress up and look good if they want to get ahead.

The flip side of *machismo* is matriarchy, and mothers and grandmothers tend to rule the roost at home, bringing up the children and managing the domestic budget, and hold down a job at the same time.

HOMOSEXUALITY IN A MACHO SOCIETY

While macho culture and the disapproval of the Catholic Church have held back gay rights across the country, things are now changing fast for the LGBT community. Government support, new laws, and progressive social media campaigns have helped to raise awareness of gay and transgender issues and establish greater levels of acceptance in Mexican society as a whole.

A liberal island in a conservative country, Mexico City has led the way on LGBT rights, legalizing same-sex marriages in 2009 and holding mass weddings in the city's main square, the Zócalo, attended by hundreds of LGBT couples from around the country. Resistance by some states in implementing a Supreme Court decision from 2015 that ruled that it was unconstitutional to refuse same-sex marriages prompted the Mexican President Enrique Peña Nieto in May 2016 to propose changes to the Constitution and Federal Civil Code to ensure equality for all Mexicans.

Annual events like Gay Pride are celebrated with carnival floats and processions over a week in June in Mexico City; and in the LGBT-friendly resort Puerto Vallarta the party, held in May, lasts twelve days.

Not everywhere in Mexico is as accepting, however, and LGBT couples have been stopped by police citing decency laws in some places for holding hands or kissing in public. In response, the LGBT community has organized a Besotón (Kissathon) and social media campaigns to highlight discrimination.

DISTRUST OF THE AUTHORITIES

There is a strong anti-establishment tendency in Mexico. Some scholars trace this lawless streak back to the Spanish Conquest, when the only protest open to the subjugated Aztecs and other indigenous Mexicans was to ignore or subvert where possible the laws of their foreign overlords. This tendency was strengthened by the many revolts and uprisings during the War of Independence, the unrest caused by the French and US invasions, the long chaos of the Mexican revolution, and the seventy-year "perfect dictatorship" under the Institutional Revolutionary Party (PRI).

A lax attitude to the rule of law is summed up by the saying "*El que no tranza, no avanza*" (essentially: "If you don't cheat, you don't get ahead"), which was employed in the satirical 1999 movie *Ley de Herodes* to expose the corrosive effects of corruption, self enrichment, and impunity on Mexico's political system and society as a whole.

Widespread disdain for the politicians and institutions tasked with implementing the law and governance, such as police, the courts, and government officials, has resulted in a beat-the-system mentality; people rely on their families and close friends for help rather than on the authorities.

In rural areas and in indigenous communities, distrust of central government has led to protest movements like the 1994 Zapatista uprising in Chiapas, which continues to this day, and the more recent vigilante groups that have sprung up to protect their towns and villages against the activities of local drug cartels.

ATTITUDES TOWARD RACE

The Spanish arrived in the New World shortly after the final push to rid Spain of the Moors following eight hundred years of Muslim rule. It was a time of great intolerance toward other faiths and saw the rise of the feared Spanish Inquisition to root out heresy. In the same year that Christopher Columbus set sail on his epic voyage, the Jews and Muslims of Spain were being forced to convert to Christianity or leave the country.

As we have seen, after conquering the Aztecs and other indigenous kingdoms, the Spanish created the rigid hierarchy known as the *casta* system. At the top were the Spanish-born *peninsulares*, followed by the *criollos* (Creoles, or locally born people of Spanish descent), *mestizos* (people of mixed Spanish and indigenous backgrounds), *Indios* (indigenous people), and, finally, black slaves from Africa.

Since Independence, Mexico has been through several periods where the country's indigenous heritage has been celebrated, especially in the 1920s and '30s when artists, writers, and archaeologists began to restore the national pride in the country's pre-Hispanic past. However, despite huge advances in social mobility, people are still judged by their skin color to a great extent.

It is also telling that the Afro-Mexican communities of Veracruz, Guerrero, and Oaxaca have only recently received any recognition. Until 2015 there was no black or African box in the national census and it was only after sustained demands from activists that a question about black ethnicity was included. As a result, 1.4 million Mexicans identified themselves as black or of African descent.

LIVING FOR THE MOMENT

In a society where the poor live from day to day, and the uncertainties of life can throw a curveball at the best laid plans, it is not surprising that people live for the moment. In rural communities and poor *barrios* of the cities, the monotony of the daily grind is broken up only by the annual cycle of festivals or family get-togethers, and people make sure they make the most of these events.

CLASS DIVISIONS

There are sharp social divisions within Mexico (40 percent of Mexicans live below the poverty line). It is only in urban areas that you find a sizeable middle class, and a working, significant-wage-earning class, between the richest and the poorest sections of society. In rural areas you are generally either one of the very few rich people or among the millions of poor. Over the past fifty years, the rich have got richer and the poor poorer. Among the latter there is an unwillingness to change and an acceptance of the status quo and their "place in society," linked to fatalism.

MEXICO AND THE USA

The nineteenth-century Mexican president Porfirio Díaz once said, "Poor Mexico, so far from God and so close to the United States." His words sum up the often difficult relationship between Mexico and its northern neighbor, which more than once has descended into armed conflict and between 1846 and 1848 resulted in the loss of nearly half of Mexico's territory.

In many ways the conflict between the two countries is a fight for the survival of Mexican culture in a world where English dominates business, Hollywood dominates movie production, and US pop is everywhere. Mexicans want to enjoy the benefits of US culture when it comes to shopping at Walmart or any of the other US chains you find in Mexico, but they don't want to lose their street markets, or their amazing culinary traditions. It's also about national pride and not being bullied, or treated like a second class citizen, by a more powerful neighbor.

Since the presidency of Barack Obama, Mexican attitudes to the US have steadily improved, especially among the young. But it only took an inflammatory statement by the US tycoon and presidential aspirant Donald Trump in 2016 to ignite a fierce storm of protest when he described Mexicans as rapists and drug dealers and said that he wanted to build a wall along the border to keep them out. The Mexicans responded to Trump in a thoroughly Mexican way, with as much satire as anger, and gleefully made *piñatas* of the tousle-haired tycoon for kids to smash, and huge papier-mâché figures of him to be burned at carnivals.

Individually, US tourists find no problems when visiting Mexico, and more than a million US citizens have moved south to set up home. If visitors show respect for Mexico and Mexican culture, and learn a few words of the lingo, Mexicans will respond with the warm hospitality for which they are famous. Pick holes in the place and come across like the stereotypical brash American, and the response won't be so welcoming.

MEXICANS IN THE USA

So many families in Mexico are affected by migration to the US that it is no surprise that there are strong feelings about the issue, and especially about the treatment of Mexicans who have made the journey across the border, both legally and illegally. Apart from the 35 million US citizens who identify as Mexican Americans, there are roughly six million Mexicans working legally in the US and an estimated six million living and working without formal papers.

The main reason for migration is economic: a chance to get a better-paid job and save up for a better life back home. Crossing the border illegally is fraught with danger, involving paid *coyotes* or *polleros* (people-smugglers) and a long trek through a hot desert that can be fatal to those not properly prepared and guided. Those who make it to the US and find a job can send money home to their families; but life for undocumented migrants is difficult: they risk arrest and deportation, have to do the lowest-paid and most menial jobs, and often go many years without seeing their families. Nevertheless, for Mexicans, the employment opportunities in the US, however badly paid, represent a safety valve for frustrations and poor prospects at home.

The increasing tensions on the border due to drug trafficking, anti-migrant vigilante groups, and the human rights abuses of Mexicans and Central American migrants by unscrupulous *polleros* are daily topics of news in Mexico.

ATTITUDES TOWARD FOREIGNERS

Few Mexicans have an opportunity to travel outside their own country, except to the US or the Caribbean, and, just as in the US, attitudes to foreigners can seem parochial and old-fashioned, sometimes falling into simplistic stereotypes. People from the Middle East and other Muslim countries are all lumped together as "Turkos"—a legacy of the days of the Ottoman Empire when Lebanese, Syrian, and Palestinian immigrants came to Mexico with Turkish papers. The Lebanese have a reputation for being good at business, and prominent Mexicans of Lebanese descent include, as we have seen, the multibillionaire Carlos Slim and the Oscar-nominated Hollywood actress and producer Salma Hayek.

East Asians are also lumped together in popular speech as *chinos* (Chinese), no matter if they come from Japan, Vietnam or Korea. A typical nickname for anybody of East Asian descent (or who has indigenous Mexican features) is El Chino or La China, often using the diminutive form *chinito* or *chinita*. A Japanese tourist might be surprised to be addressed in a market with a friendly: "*Hola, chinito. En que te puedo ayudar?*" ("Hi, little Chinese person. How can I help you?")

Mexicans are genuinely interested to meet foreign visitors to their country and will try out their English—and put your Spanish vocabulary to the test—to find out more about you and your country, especially about the food you eat, how much people earn, and what the weather's like. These are great conversation starters, and will generally lead to questions about your opinions of Mexico. Keep conversations light and stick to positive impressions, and you may make a friend.

You may find that people stare at you on public transport or in the street for longer than you would expect at home. Don't be alarmed; it's only curiosity.

BEACH ETIQUETTE

A Catholic country with a conservative attitude to how much flesh should be on display at the beach, and decency laws that should be respected, Mexico is not a place where topless or nude bathing is widespread.

You will find resorts in Cabo, Puerto Vallarta, and Playa del Carmen with a more relaxed attitude to beach attire, and even the odd isolated beach popular with naturists, but bear in mind that anywhere that attracts families with children is less likely to tolerate toplessness and always ask locals before you dare to bare.

Also, when visiting beach towns, cover up with a T-shirt and long shorts or trousers before entering a local church, bank, or market. It is seen as disrespectful to step into a place of worship in a bikini or a pair of speedos.

MEXICAN HUMOR

Clever wordplay, a creative use of puns, and earthy double meanings are key elements of Mexican humor. Movie legend Mario Moreno Reyes, better known as Cantinflas, was a great slapstick artist with instinctive comic timing, who typically played the underdog, the *mestizo* country boy in the big city with just his wits and fast tongue to get by. The true power of his performances came from his ability to tie up his onscreen rivals—especially pompous authority figures—in comic knots. Cantinflas had the common touch, the humor of the *barrio*, where verbal dexterity is highly prized. You find the same humor in the songs of Chava Flores and in the hugely successful

TV show "El Chavo del Ocho," created by the much loved comedian, actor, and writer Roberto Gómez Bolaños, whose stage name, Chesperito, comes from "Little Shakespeare." Another iconic comedic figure of Mexican cinema is German Valdés, or Tin Tan, whose comedy came in part from mixing Mexican slang with the "Spanglish" used by Mexican Americans.

Jokes in Mexico often hinge on double meanings, known as *albur*, which can have sexual connotations. Affectionate abuse or banter that employs *albures* is typical among friends. There are even *albur* competitions, like verbal fencing matches, where contestants take it in turns to come up with witty putdowns until one is left without a reply.

While Mexicans will find comedy in every situation, and are quick to mock, they are very sensitive to foreigners making fun of them or of anything they hold dear. By all means join in with the joshing, and take the banter on the chin with a smile, but don't make a joke about the Mexican football team or the Virgin of Guadalupe.

CUSTOMS & TRADITIONS

With a dizzying whirl of religious festivals, carnivals, and national commemorations crammed into Mexico's annual calendar, you can rest assured that on any given day at least one small town somewhere will be decked out in colorful bunting as the locals prepare to party.

The majority of these festivals are linked to the calendar of Catholic religious observances

brought from Spain by the conquistadors. Following the fall of the Aztec capital Tenochtitlán, Spanish priests zealously imposed Roman Catholicism on the indigenous people they subjugated, introducing a cycle of moveable feasts and saints' days into the *mestizo* melting pot of conquest. However, travel around and you will find countless vestiges of pre-Hispanic belief and ritual conserved in the country's colorful celebrations.

Mexico's tumultuous history is also remembered through the year, with the celebration of important dates such as the Grito de Dolores (Cry of Dolores), marking Padre Miguel Hidalgo's momentous 1810 call for Mexican independence from Spain.

Joyous Explosions

Mexico's most famous man of letters, the poet Octavio Paz, wrote that Mexico's many festivals are like a pressure valve, making life bearable for Mexico's poor and downtrodden. "Our fiestas are explosions," he wrote. "There is nothing so joyous as a Mexican fiesta, but there is also nothing so sorrowful. Life and death, joy and sorrow, music and mere noise are united."

FESTIVALS AND HOLIDAYS

Mexicans love to party, and take their festivals very seriously, with newspapers publishing the upcoming holidays at the start of the year so that families can start to plan their vacations. There are several types of holiday throughout the year. *Días Feriados*, also known as *Días de Asueto*, are statutory public holidays, where workers get a day off, or extra pay for working.

Civic holidays, such as Día del Ejército (Army Day) and Día de la Bandera (Flag Day), are celebrated nationally but don't include a mandatory day off (although some local government offices close).

Some religious holidays, such as Carnaval (Carnival) and Semana Santa (Easter) are moveable feasts that fall on different dates each year and can last upward of a week. Others, such as Día de los Fieles Difuntos (Day of the Dead, November 2) fall on fixed dates when banks and government offices will generally be closed, but may also be extended over several days.

Expect heavy traffic in peak holiday times or during local festivals, when it is best to avoid travel unless you plan to participate, in which case arrange transportation and accommodation well in advance.

PUBLIC HOLIDAYS

January 1	Año Nuevo (New Year's Day)
First Monday in February	Día de la Constitución (Constitution Day)
Third Monday in March	Benito Juárez's birthday
March–April	Jueves Santo (Maundy Thursday)
	Viernes Santo (Good Friday)
	Semana Santa (Easter)
May 1	Día del Trabajo (Labor Day)
September 16	Día de la Independencia (Independence Day)
Third Monday in November	Día de la Revolución (Revolution Day)
December 25	Navidad (Christmas Day)

THE FESTIVAL CALENDAR
January 1: Año Nuevo
New Year's Eve is traditionally celebrated at home with music, dancing, drinking, and a big family meal, much like Christmas dinner. B*acalao* (salted cod) and *pavo* (turkey) are typically served at this time of year, and *pozole* (hominy stew made with pork or chicken) is also popular. The celebrations culminate with a glass of sparkling wine or cider and twelve grapes, which must be eaten during the twelve chimes of midnight. New Year rituals include sweeping the house to get rid of bad luck, putting on new clothes to start afresh, taking a suitcase into the street to increase the chances of travel,

and wearing colored underwear (red for love, yellow for money, and white for peace and health). The night ends with a bang, as fireworks fill the skies and people party into the early hours.

January 6: El Dia de Reyes

Called Epiphany in English, this day celebrates the arrival of the Three Kings, Caspar, Melchior, and Balthasar, in Bethlehem with gifts of gold, frankincense, and myrrh for the baby Jesus. Many Mexican children still get their presents on this day rather than at Christmas.

A SWEET TRADITION FOR THE THREE KINGS

Rosca de Reyes is a sweet oval bread with a hole in the center that represents a crown, with dried fruit for the encrusted jewels and a small figure of the Baby Jesus baked into it. Traditionally, it is shared with friends and family on January 6, the Día de los Reyes (Three Kings' Day). The *rosca* is typically served with a cup of hot chocolate and *tamales*. Everybody waits to see who will get the slice containing the Baby Jesus, as that person has to provide *tamales* for all on February 2 (Candlemas).

February 14: Día de San Valentín

Valentine's Day isn't just about anonymous love letters, flowers, chocolates, romantic dinners, and mariachi serenades. It's also known as Día de la Amistad (Friendship Day), and Mexicans will also celebrate the day with friends.

February 24: Día de la Bandera de Mexico

Mexican Flag Day celebrates the day in 1821 that Agustín de Iturbide unfurled the tricolor flag for the first time, with a green stripe representing hope, white for unity, and red for the blood spilled by Mexico's independence heroes. The coat of arms in the center is inspired by the Aztec legend of the founding of Tenochtitlán by the nomadic Mexica, after the sun god Huitzilopochtli told them to settle where they found an eagle perched on a prickly pear, devouring a snake.

February/March: Carnaval

Carnival is the last big blowout before the privations of Lent, and is celebrated on a grand scale with parties, parades, beauty queens, marching bands, floats, fireworks, and costumed revels. The colorful chaos continues day and night with non-stop dancing, drinking. and revelers throwing water and *cascarones*—eggshells filled with confetti. The biggest celebrations are held in Mazatlán in Sinaloa, Veracruz on the Gulf coast, Baja California, and Mérida in Yucatán.

March/April: Semana Santa

Holy Week is one of the biggest vacations of the year. It is in fact a two-week holiday, and Mexicans head off en masse to beaches and picturesque towns, to visit relatives, or to attend the processions, masses, and passion plays that reenact the crucifixion and

resurrection of Jesus Christ in full gory detail on Jueves Santo (Maundy Thursday) and Viernes Santo (Good Friday). On Sábado de Gloria (Easter Saturday) large papier-mâché effigies representing unpopular politicians or figures of ridicule are filled with fireworks and gleefully exploded in the "*quema de Judas*" (burning of Judas). In many places, such as Oaxaca and Chiapas, indigenous and Catholic beliefs and rituals come together in spectacles of costume, prayer, and dance. The elaborate Teguinada celebrations of the

Tarahumara (Rarámuri) of Copper Canyon combine mock battles between horned Pharisees and Roman soldiers with ancient fertility and rain rituals that involve the Sun and Moon gods, shamanism, dancing around the church to the sounds of violin and drums, and gallons of *tesgüino* (maize beer).

April 25: Feria de San Marcos

This is a huge state fair in Aguascalientes that starts a week before St. Mark's Day and continues for another two weeks. The festival is famous for its cockfights, bullfights, *charreadas* (rodeos), and performances by Mexico's top performers, particularly mariachi stars.

May 5: Cinco de Mayo

Not to be confused with Mexican Independence Day. In Mexico, celebrations mainly take place in Puebla, where on May 5, 1862, a poorly equipped Mexican force led by General Ignacio Zaraoza defeated an invading French army that was marching on Mexico City from Veracruz.

May 10: Día de la Madre

Mother's Day is a big event, given the importance of the family, with mothers receiving cards, flowers, and even treats at work.

May/June, First Thursday after Trinity Sunday: Corpus Christi

This Catholic feast day celebrates the consecration of the Eucharist as the body and blood of Christ. Processions take place all over the country, and firework towers called *castillos* add to the festive atmosphere. A popular tradition in Puebla is to buy *mulitas* (little models of mules) and to dress children in indigenous costumes. In Papantla, in Veracruz state, death-defying *voladores* (flyers) continue a pre-Columbian tradition linked to fertility rituals and sun worship. Groups of five men climb a high pole and while one sits at the top and plays a flute the other four spin around the pole attached only by a rope tied around their waists. The *voladores* descend gradually as they circle the pole, each flyer making thirteen revolutions for a total of fifty-two, representing the 52-year cycle of the Mesoamerican calendar.

June 1: Día de la Marina
Navy Day is celebrated with military parades in port towns.

July, last two Mondays: Guelaguetza
A major folk and handicrafts festival, Guelaguetza takes place in Oaxaca and harks back to a pre-Columbian maize festival dedicated to the goddess Centeotl. A riot of color, it features regional folk dances, the election of a "goddess" rather than a beauty queen, and a reenactment of the life of the last Zapotec princess, Donají.

September 16: Independence Day
Independence Day is a national holiday with parades, fireworks, and traditional music in celebration of the "Grito de Dolores" (Cry of Dolores), Padre Miguel Hidalgo's call for Mexican independence from Spain in 1810. In a televised address from the balcony of the Palacio Nacional at 11:00 p.m. every September 15, the president of the day reenacts the Grito in front of a huge crowd in Mexico City's main square, the Zocalo, by unfurling the Mexican flag, ringing the Dolores bell, and calling out the names of independence heroes: "*Viva Hidalgo! Viva Morelos! Viva Josefa Ortiz de Domínguez!*

Viva Allende! Vivan Aldama y Matamoros! Viva la independencia nacional! Viva México! Viva México! Viva México!"

October 12: Día de la Raza
Still celebrated in some states as *Descubrimiento de América* (Discovery of America Day), this marks Christopher Columbus' arrival in the Americas in 1492. Nowadays, indigenous Mexican groups use the day to highlight their struggle for land rights or raise awareness of the achievements of Mexico's pre-Columbian civilizations, such as the Olmecs, Aztecs, and Mayans.

October: Festival Internacional Cervantino
This, the biggest arts festival in Mexico, takes place in Guanajuato in central Mexico. Theater groups, dance troupes, and musicians come from around the world.

October 31–November 2: Día de los Muertos, or Hanal Pixan
The Day of the Dead is the defining Mexican festival, and certainly the most visually arresting. It begins on the night of October 31. The belief is that the dead have

divine permission to visit friends and relatives on earth
once a year, and they are welcomed with offerings of
food and flowers between this date and November 2.
Salt and water, or the favorite meal of the dead person,
may be left out for the spirit to come down and "eat."
Candles and incense are burned in graveyards, and
tombs are decorated with flowers, but this is no somber
occasion. History has given Mexicans a familiarity
with death that is perhaps beyond the usual Western
comfort zone: it is both mocked and celebrated.
The skulls and skeletons displayed everywhere are
a uniquely Mexican artifact. They are spectacular,
amusing, and made of any material imaginable, from
tin to chocolate.

December 12: Día de la Virgen de Guadalupe

The Feast of the Virgin of Guadalupe brings tens
of thousands of pilgrims from all over the world
to worship at the Basílica de Nuestra Señora de
Guadalupe. Some come in indigenous dress, others
in simple smocks, and many inch their way on their
knees, rosaries in hand, to show their devotion. A
modern circular church built in 1974 houses the
original image of the dark haired, brown-skinned

Virgin Mary that miraculously appeared on the *tilma* (tunic) of an Aztec convert to Catholicism called Juan Diego in 1531 (see page 68). The image of the Virgin of Guadalupe is without doubt the holiest relic in Mexico and all of Latin America, inspiring both the devotion and the fervent patriotism of the Mexican people.

So many pilgrims come to see the revered image that the basilica has been fitted with a series of moving walkways, conveyor belts to speed the faithful along as they snap away on their smartphones.

While pilgrims visit the old basilica with its subsiding, wonky walls, and the chapel on the hill where the second apparition took place, dancers and musicians dressed in Aztec garb called *concheros* bring a splash of pre-Columbian spectacle to the huge plaza.

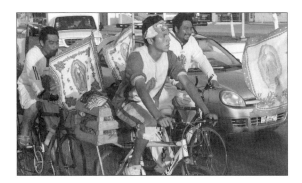

December 16–24: Posadas

These are candlelit family and church processions
that mark the start of Christmas with a reenactment

of the story of Joseph
and Mary, who arrived
in Bethlehem and had to
knock on doors to find
a *posada* (guesthouse).
People sing *villancicos*
(Christmas carols) as they
go from house to house
in the neighborhood and
processions traditionally
culminate with a *piñata*, a
papier-mâché figure filled
with sweets and hung
from a rope. Children are
blindfolded and take turns to bash at the *piñata* with a
stick until it breaks and the sweets are released.

December 24 and 25: Navidad

Christmas is a time when Mexican families gather to
eat together, share presents, and set off some fireworks.
Noche Buena (Christmas Eve) is the main celebration,
with many families attending a mass in the church —
including a late *misa de gallo* (midnight mass)—and
singing *villancicos*. Christmas dinner is eaten late, and
varies around the country from traditional *bacalao*
(salted cod) and *guajolote* (turkey) to *lechón* (suckling
pig). Other dishes include corn dough *tamales* and an
Aztec dish called *romeritos,* a stringy rosemary-like herb
that is cooked like spinach and served in a *mole* sauce
with shrimp patties. Drinks include wine, beer, cider,
and *ponche*, a hot fruit punch with cinnamon. Presents
are generally given on Christmas Eve, although, as
mentioned above, many children still receive their main

presents on January 6. Christmas Day is spent visiting family, relaxing, and eating *recalentado*—reheated leftovers from the big blowout the day before.

December 28: Día de los Santos Inocentes

The Day of the Holy Innocents is so-called because of the biblical story of King Herod ordering the massacre of children under two years in Bethlehem in a vain attempt to kill the baby Jesus. Now it's a day to prey on the innocent and gullible with jokes and pranks, like April Fool's Day in the US and the UK.

Happy Saint's Day

There's a saint in the Catholic calendar for every day of the year, and in the past people were named after the *santo* (saint) whose feast day they were born on. Nowadays, names are more loosely tied to the Church, but people still receive cards, small gifts, or just a phone call from their family to wish them well on their saint's day, as if it were a second birthday.

SAINTS' DAYS AND PILGRIMAGES

Towns and villages around Mexico will generally have at least one celebration to honor the patron saint of their church. Saints' days are also celebrated with pilgrimages to their shrines. San Antonio Abad is the patron saint of animals. On his feast day, January 17, people come to churches with dogs, cats, sheep, calves, hamsters, goldfish, even iguanas, so the priests can sprinkle holy water on the pets. In Taxco, Guerrero State, the church service culminates with a contest for the animal with the best costume. The most important pilgrimage in Mexico culminates on December 12 at the Basilica of Our Lady of Guadalupe, the patron saint of Mexico.

MIRACULOUS MANIFESTATION OF OUR LADY OF GUADALUPE

The spiritual heart of Mexico, and the country's most important pilgrimage site, is the shrine to Nuestra Señora de Guadalupe (Our Lady of Guadalupe), an enormous modern basilica on the outskirts of Mexico City. The main focus of devotion is a venerated image of the Virgin Mary that miraculously appeared on the *tilma* (agave-fiber cloak) of a Nahua-speaking native called Juan Diego de Cuautitlán on December 9, 1531.

As the story goes, the Holy Mother appeared to Juan Diego as he was passing the hill of Tepeyac, which coincidentally housed a shrine to the Aztec mother goddess Tonantzin. To calm the astonished Aztec after appearing before him in a burst of radiant light, the Virgin Mary reportedly said: "Do not be afraid. Am I not here, I who am your mother?" She then told Juan Diego to instruct the local bishop to build a church on the site in her honor, but the bishop ignored him. The Virgin then appeared again on December 12, telling Juan Diego to pick flowers from the hill and take them to the bishop. When the astonished bishop saw the beautiful flowers and an image of the Virgin imprinted on the *tilma* he was convinced that Juan Diego's story was true and the first shrine to Our Lady of Guadalupe was built in 1533.

Some investigators have cast doubt on the miracle, suggesting the story of Juan Diego and the radiant Virgin was just a myth cooked up by the Catholic clergy to speed up the conversion of the indigenous population. They point out that the name Guadalupe comes from the Virgin of Guadalupe in Extremadura, Spain, the place where Hernán Cortés and many of his fellow conquistadors were born. Despite the naysayers, Juan Diego became the first indigenous saint from the Americas when he was beatified by Pope John Paul II in 2002, and the Basilica of Our Lady of Guadalupe continues to be the most visited Catholic shrine on the planet.

"WITCHCRAFT" AND SUPERSTITION

Many superstitions are found in Mexico, a legacy of the country's melting pot of cultural traditions. Some superstitions came with the Spanish from Europe; some from the Catholic Church; others derive from the beliefs and rituals of Mexico's pre-Columbian past and surviving indigenous groups. Mexicans share the belief that black cats bring bad luck, and that thirteen is an unlucky number—although the day to dread is Martes 13 (Tuesday 13), not Friday 13. In keeping with Catholic tradition, people will typically make the sign of the cross rather than cross their fingers when they want to positively influence the outcome of an event or stave off some impending disaster.

Brujería (witchcraft) in Mexico is not about old crones on broomsticks but an important element of daily life. Walk into any market in Mexico and you will find stalls selling herbs, candles, and perfumes guaranteed to bring you love, success, and happiness, and others to counteract the *envidia* (envy) of others.

There is a widespread belief, especially in rural and indigenous communities, in *mal de ojo* (the evil eye), a type of curse that can bring bad luck or ill health, especially to children. Amulets of red beads or coral are worn to protect against *mal de ojo,* and children thought to be suffering from its effects are taken to see folk healers and shamans who use incense, tobacco smoke, and incantations to cure them. One home remedy is the *limpia de huevo* (egg cleansing), in which an egg is rubbed all over the child's body and then cracked into a bowl that is left under the child's bed overnight to absorb all the bad energy.

Curanderos (spiritual healers), *brujos* (witches), and shamans practice their arts all over Mexico. Some work in clinics, like doctors, others employ ancient rituals in places of power, such as waterfalls, or at archaeological sites. In Chiapas, the local Tzotzil Maya shamans of San Juan Chamula practice healing rituals that combine Catholic elements with Mayan rituals involving copal incense and a local liquor called *pox* (pronounced "posh") to achieve trance states that allow them to diagnose and cure the spiritual ills affecting the patient's two souls.

In the north of Mexico, the isolation of the Huichol people of the Sierra Madre Mountains has helped to preserve their complex spiritual beliefs and rituals. Their rich symbolism, involving the sun god and his eagle wife, corn, deer, snakes, and fire, is expressed in brightly colored weavings that are highly prized by collectors. The Huichol have a reputation as great healers and employ the hallucinogenic peyote cactus to open the way to the spirit realm.

NARCO SAINTS

Not all spiritual practices in Mexico are positive. Among the many religious statues on sale in markets and street stalls you will come across images of so-called "Narco Saints," like the Santa Muerte, a skeletal women draped in a long cloak, and Jesus Malverde, a Robin Hood-like folk saint from Sinaloa with a matinée-idol moustache. Criminals pray to these saints to give them protection from the authorities and their enemies; poor Mexicans living in areas with high crime rates pray to them for protection from criminals.

chapter four

MAKING FRIENDS

Mexicans are friendly, gregarious, and like to socialize in groups. Families are large in Mexico and family ties are strong, so most Mexicans have a social circle that centers on the home, the extended family, and neighbors. Non-family friends and workmates may be invited home for birthday parties or to family events like christenings and weddings, but generally people meet up with friends in bars and restaurants, or at a picnic in the park.

Foreigners working in Mexico will find that their Mexican colleagues are quick to invite them for an after-work drink or a meal out, which is a good first step for making friends.

An invitation home to meet the family is quite a big deal. If you turn it down you could offend. Make sure to take a gift, like a decent bottle of tequila or wine, and keep in mind that all attempts you make to speak Spanish, try new foods, join in with the dancing, and generally have fun will be greatly appreciated. Stand on ceremony, or stubbornly refuse entreaties to join in the karaoke or limbo dancing, and you risk being labeled an *aguafiestas* (killjoy, or party pooper).

EXPAT FRIENDLY

Mexico came second only to Ecuador in a 2015 survey carried out by InterNations, an international networking group, aimed at finding the best (and worst) places for expatriates. Mexico got top marks for ease of settling in to the local culture, and came second in the subcategories for friendliness and finding friends. In total, 70 percent of the expats surveyed agreed that making local friends is easy, and 37 percent said they mostly make new friends by meeting people from their local neighborhood.

Mexico also scored highly on the cost of living, but did poorly on working hours (too long), job security (not enough), and personal safety (could be better). Of the sixty-one countries included in the survey, Ecuador, Mexico, and Malta came top.

THE LANGUAGE BARRIER

One of the biggest problems facing newcomers in Mexico is the language barrier. A lack of conversational Spanish can sap your spontaneity and smother your style. A night out can seem stilted when you are limited to set phrases, frantic miming, or resorting to translation apps. Ever hospitable, Mexicans will

still include you in social events and try to explain
expressions and jokes, but it's harder to click with people
when you don't have the lingo. Spanish classes will not
only give you confidence, new vocabulary, and feedback
on your delivery, but also provide a place to make friends
with fellow learners and a teacher who can fill you in on
local culture, cool places to eat, and popular hangouts.

THINK LOCAL

Foreigners sometimes complain that it's hard to meet
people in Mexico, and that they have few acquaintances
in their building or neighborhood. Do what the Mexicans
do and make a point of saying *"Buenos días!"* or *"Buenas
tardes!"* to your neighbors, the guy in the newspaper
kiosk, and the girl on the juice stand. Introduce yourself,
ask people their names, and remember them for next
time. Before you know it you'll be up to speed on the
local gossip and might even get a nickname.

FASHIONABLY LATE

When it comes to social engagements, British punctuality
will not win you any friends. Turn up to a party on the
dot, and you are likely to find the Mexican girl who
invited you is still doing her hair and is not amused at
having to entertain you while she finishes getting dressed.
Whatever the occasion—even weddings, christenings,
and funerals—people tend to turn up at least half an hour
late. This tardiness is such a fact of life that if you really
want people to turn up at 8:00 p.m. you invite them for
7:30. Even so, you should still expect some of your guests
to show up after 9:00. Equally, when out on a date wait
at least twenty minutes past the arranged time before
sending a terse text. The secret is to go with the flow and
relax into a more Mexican concept of time.

What's In A Nickname?

A lot of Mexican humor is based on witty wordplay and *double entendre*, and Mexicans get playful with people's names. First there are the short forms: Pancho or Paco is Francisco, Memo is Guillermo, Lalo is Eduardo, Chucho or Chuy is Jesus, Chepe is José, Lupe or Lupita is Guadalupe, Conchita is Concepción, and Cuca is María del Refugio.

If that isn't confusing enough, almost everybody in Mexico has a nickname (*apodo*), usually given to them at school and generally with the intention of poking fun at them. Sometimes the names are ironic, so the skinniest guy in the group will be called "El Gordo" (Fatty) and the best-looking "El Feo" (ugly). But usually nicknames are literal, and can sometimes come across as politically incorrect to US or UK ears, especially when the fairest girl in the group is called "La Güerita" (Little Blondie), the one with Amerindian features "La Chinita" (Little Chinese Girl), the darkest girl "La Negra" (Black), and the slimmest "La Calaca" (Skeleton). And then there are Mexico's most famous drug lords. The diminutive Joaquin Guzman is known to the word as "El Chapo" (Shorty, from *chaparro*), the fearsome Óscar Guerrero was rather bizarrely called "El Winnie Pooh," and Amado Carrillo Fuentes had the grand moniker of "El Señor de los Cielos" (Lord of the Skies).

CONVERSATION STARTERS AND STOPPERS

Mexicans like to keep things light and jocular when socializing and will seek common ground, asking you about your family, your favorite music, food, beer, and what you think about Mexico. This is not an invitation to launch into a list of the things you think are wrong with the country. People in Mexico are very proud of their country and are sensitive to criticism of it, especially given its difficult history with the US. While locals might gripe about the pollution levels in Mexico City, the surreal absurdity of the latest political scandal, and the tragic human toll of the war on drugs, they may not appreciate a foreign visitor doing the same.

EXPAT GROUPS

With multinationals employing thousands of foreign workers in Mexico City, Guadalajara, and Monterrey, and more than a million US citizens resident in the country, one way to widen your social circle is to join an expat group. Retirement havens like Ajijic on Lake Chapala and San Miguel de Allende have a full calendar of activities and cultural events in English and Spanish. In the Yucatán, and resort towns like Ensenada, Playas de Rosarito, and Puerto Vallarta the local expat communities are swollen by "snowbirds" in winter months, and you'll have no trouble finding English-language activities to ease you into local living.

The international social networking group InterNations has chapters in Mexico City, Guadalajara, and Monterrey, and offers young and not so young expats the opportunity to meet up with old hands and locals at cocktail evenings, brunch meetings, taco tastings, sporting events, and cinema nights. Another international networking site in Mexico is MeetUp.com, which is a great place to find groups organizing a host of events and activities from book groups to chess clubs, language exchanges, and Latin dance nights.

THE DATING GAME

If navigating the language can be tricky in a foreign land, *buscando amor* (trying to find love), with all the cultural nuances involved, can be a minefield. In Mexico, the love game is still quite traditional, with macho men expected to treat the objects of their passion with effusive declarations of undying love, gifts of flowers and chocolates, and unexpected mariachi serenades.

This old-school attitude is reflected in the general courtesies and gallantry shown to women: opening doors for them, paying for everything on a night out, and making sure they are delivered safely to their door. The downside to all this romance can be manifested in soap-opera sensitivities, possessiveness, jealousy, and a poor response to rejection (just listen to the words of most mariachi songs).

In big towns and cities younger Mexicans are increasingly looking for love via their smartphones on apps like Tinder. Dating Web sites can also be an effective way to line up dates, but steer clear of those that specifically want to hook up locals with foreigners, as motives might be purely financial. The best way to *ligar* (hook up) is probably to follow the same advice for finding friends. Mexicans are always happy to match-make, and if you build up a group of friends from work, expat connections, or networking sites they will soon start introducing you to possible soul mates. This can work well, as going out in a group takes the pressure out of that first date, and will expand your social circle.

THE MEXICANS AT HOME

Mexican homes are as varied as the Mexicans who inhabit them. They range from the luxury penthouses with swimming pools and servants of the urban mega-rich, to the spacious, Spanish-style *haciendas* of rural landowners. For the middle class there are the gentrified *colonias* (neighborhoods) of two- or three-story houses in the hearts of the cities, apartments in shiny skyscrapers offering all mod cons, or new-build suburbs on the outskirts. A working-class family might rent a high-rise concrete apartment in one of the vast social-housing projects constructed in the 1970s, while the urban poor are crammed into the sprawling *ciudades perdidas* (shanty towns) that encircle the country's major cities. In the Yucatán, the Maya still build distinctive single-story oval houses with adobe walls and thatched roofs that have changed little in centuries.

THE RISE OF THE CITIES

Since the 1900s there has been a steady movement
from the countryside to urban centers. In 1900 only
10 percent of the population lived in cities, but the
balance started to shift with the upheavals of the
Mexican Revolution in 1910 and the later moves
to industrialize the economy. Nowadays, some
80 percent of Mexicans live in cities, the majority
of them in the country's four main urban centers—
Mexico City, Guadalajara, Puebla, and Monterrey—
and in the border towns of Juárez and Tijuana.

The main magnet for those looking to improve
their lives is still the behemoth that is Mexico City,
which has expanded to absorb so many of the
surrounding towns and suburbs that the Mexico City
Metropolitan Area now has a population of over
21 million people, making it the largest metropolitan
area in the Western Hemisphere, the tenth-largest
city on the planet, and the largest Spanish-speaking
city in the world. The city also encompasses the
Neza-Chalco-Itza shanty town, which with four
million inhabitants is considered the largest slum
in the world.

MOTHER KNOWS BEST

Mexico has a reputation as a macho country, but at the heart of the family and the home is generally a mother or grandmother who holds everything together. Although things are slowly changing, women still have responsibility for overseeing the cooking, cleaning, and childcare, even if they hold down a full-time job. Many women will also manage the family budget: paying bills, doing the weekly shopping, and organizing family events such as Christmas, birthdays, and christenings.

This matriarchal set-up is deeply rooted in Mexican culture and is important in a country where historically many fathers have had to work away from the family home for long periods. The strong national devotion to Mexico's patron saint, Our Lady of Guadalupe, also known as the Holy Mother, is a reflection of the reverence in which mothers are held.

While "Your mother" jokes might be popular in the US, you insult a Mexican's mother at your peril.

HOME HELP

From the uniformed maids, nannies, chauffeurs, and gardeners of the mega-rich to the lady who comes in once a week to clean up and help a working mother with the ironing, many people in Mexico have some sort of home help. Most professionals will have someone who comes and cleans once a week or more, and very often they will run errands, wash clothes, and cook a meal as well.

For the rich and upper-middle class, having servants is seen as a status symbol. Live-in maids are a luxury that many can afford as they are generally paid less than the minimum wage in return for room and board. Some of them will have worked in a family for years, and will have built up a relationship with several generations. Employers might pay for the education of a maid's children, or might give them parties on their birthdays.

Relationships are not always so benevolent, and there are rights groups in Mexico calling for domestic workers to be better protected under labor laws, with minimum wages, regulated hours of work, statutory time off, paid holidays, and pension provisions.

Home help, in the form of maids, nannies, and cooks, is something to which expats moving to Mexico have to adapt. Generally, Mexicans argue that employing domestic workers is a way of helping people who would otherwise be underemployed. There are agencies that specialize in finding domestic workers and will provide references from past employers, but many people rely on recommendations from friends and coworkers.

The best way to address your domestic helpers is by their names. It's important to be aware that some of the terms used to describe such people are considered derogatory. Many Mexicans will refer to *la empleada* (the hired help), but *la muchacha* or *la 'chacha* (the girl), especially when applied to a mature woman in her forties or fifties, can seem patronizing, and *la sirvienta* (the servant) sounds inappropriate nowadays. Most offensive and definitely avoided are *la gata* (the cat), and *la criada* (literally, "raised"), dating back to the time when a family would take in a poor girl as young as ten or twelve to work in their home.

SOAP OPERA SERVANTS

Uniformed maids are a mainstay of Mexico's popular *telenovelas* (soap operas), either as the main characters, or involved in the subplots and intrigues. In the 1960s the rise of maids as protagonists in long-running TV dramas like *Maria Isabel* reflected the growing number of poor young women, many of them from indigenous cultures, who came to the capital to work in the houses of the wealthy.

Afternoon timeslots for the *telenovelas* were tweaked so that domestic workers could tune in while taking a break between cleaning up after lunch and serving dinner.

Many soap operas have reworked the simplistic Cinderella tale of a poor servant girl who finds happiness in the arms of the handsome son of a wealthy family, but the reality is rarely so romantic. Mexico's live-in maids work long hours for low pay, get no paid holidays or pension, live far from their families, and more often than not have no written contract outlining their duties, hours, or salary, leaving them open to exploitation.

DAILY LIFE

Forget the stereotype of a sombrero-wearing Mexican stretched out in the shade, calmly watching the world go by. Daily life for most Mexicans involves a hectic schedule, juggling work and family commitments, a few hours on public transport commuting across town, and a fair dose of socializing when the sun goes down.

Mexico's middle class has grown dramatically over the last twenty years to about 35–40 percent of the population, but another 40 percent still live in poverty, and the gulf between the "haves" and the "have nots," especially in rural areas, continues to pose a problem for Mexican society. As a consequence, days start very early for many people and can finish very late.

Wherever Mexicans live, food plays an important role and is generally still made from scratch. For many wives and mothers the first task of the day involves cooking corn tortillas on a griddle, and making coffee to have with *pan dulce* (sweet rolls). A light *desayuno*

(breakfast) at home is usually supplemented by a street snack or *antojito* (literally, "little craving"), such as *gorditas*, *quesadillas*, or *tacos de nopal* (cactus paddle tacos). For a more substantial breakfast, maybe at the weekend after a big night out, Mexicans will have *chilaquiles*, made of crunchy fried tortilla triangles cooked in a spicy tomato sauce and topped with cheese, or *huevos rancheros*, with a couple of fried eggs on tortillas topped with refried beans and a salsa. A Yucatán variation called *huevos motuleños* also includes ham, peas, and plantains with the spicy salsa and corn tortillas for a full blowout.

The working day can start as early as 5:00 a.m. for those who have to commute long distances or set up stalls in markets, and offices generally start work at around 8:00 to 8:30 a.m. By 10:30 or 11:00 a.m. it's time for *almuerzo*—either coffee with *pan dulce* or more *antojitos*.

Lunch, known as *comida* or *comida fuerte* (literally, "heavy meal"), is usually the main meal of the day and is often eaten at *taquerías* (*taco* stands) or small restaurants called *fondas* or *loncherías* that serve set-menu lunches at cheap prices.

In the countryside the day finishes earlier for many people, but in cities offices close by about 7:00 p.m. and a light *cena* (evening meal) is eaten late, at 8:00–9:00 p.m. either at home with the family, or out at a food stall, bar, or restaurant with friends or workmates. Inviting friends back home to eat with the family is not usual, so if you do get an invitation you can feel quite privileged.

On weekends, after drinks at bars or *cantinas*, the late-night action usually ends up at a *taquería* or street stall serving *antojitos*.

EVERYDAY SHOPPING

In the big cities you can easily find shiny supermarkets and US chains like Walmart and Costco, but most people in Mexico continue to do their food shopping in large covered markets or at local street stalls.

The markets offer a chance to chat with stallholders and try the food before you buy. The colorful piles of chili peppers, vegetables, exotic fruit, and cuts of meat on sale stimulate the senses and offer inspiration to jaded cooks. Markets are also some of the best places to enjoy a fruit juice or a traditional Mexican dish. Sit-down food stalls sell a range of *antojitos, comidas*, and favorites like *posole* (hominy and pork soup), *tlayudas* (a Oaxacan tortilla dish sometimes described as

"Mexican pizza"), and *chapulines* (fried grasshoppers). Mexicans will organize their week around the shops and markets they visit, often buying particular items on particular days, and picking up whatever's in season or on special offer.

In Mexico City the huge Mercado la Merced has one of the biggest ranges of market food in the country and is also a good place to pick up mops, brooms, and buckets. Nearby is the sprawling Mercado de Sonora, known by locals as the *mercado de los brujos* (witches' market). People come here for the eclectic selection of medicinal herbs, potions, amulets, religious icons, colored candles, and various strange and spooky items. You can get your palm read, have aromatic incense wafted over you to banish evil spirits, and pick up a perfume that makes you irresistible to the opposite sex. Bizarrely, for a market full of icons of the Santa Muerte, people also come here to buy children's toys, costumes, and *piñatas*.

EDUCATION

Having a good education is highly prized in Mexico. Public schools are free to all from six to fifteen years of age, but standards in the state education sector vary considerably, especially in rural areas, and there is a significant dropout rate.

Another factor affecting public schools is the teachers' union, the Sindicato Nacional de Trabajadores de la Educación (SNTE), which has some 1.4 million members and ranks as one of the most powerful trade unions in Latin America. Corruption charges have dogged union leaders, and protests by teachers and disputes with breakaway unions have slowed the pace of educational reform.

Some parents make huge sacrifices to send their children to private schools to improve their future prospects. These can range from small, one-room schools in rural areas to grand colleges where the kids are dropped off by chauffeurs and nannies. At the top are *colegios bilingues* (bilingual schools), which teach in English as well as Spanish and cater to the children of the elite and expats.

In most towns and cities you will find a profusion of private schools and colleges catering to working adults who return to education in their twenties and thirties. These colleges offer night school classes in English, law, accountancy, hairdressing, and dentistry.

For middle- and upper-class Mexicans, attending a good school, getting a place at a good university, and doing a Masters or MBA abroad are seen as the keys to a good career.

The School System

Compulsory free education in the public school system currently starts in *primaria* (primary school) for children from six to twelve, although there are plans to extend it to pre-school for three- and four-year-olds.

Secundaria (Secondary School or Junior High) is from thirteen to fifteen, and is also obligatory. *Prepa* (short for *preparatoria*) is the equivalent of High School, and prepares students for entry into a university or technical college. This level is not compulsory; the reality is that most young people leave at the end of secondary school, and some before that.

Both public and private schools have to follow the curriculum laid down by the SEP (Secretaría de Educación Pública, the Public Education Ministry) and the 8:00 a.m. to 1:00 p.m. school day, but private schools generally offer extra subjects and will often have a longer school day, or after-school classes extending into the afternoon.

LEARNING ENGLISH

Given Mexico's long shared border with its English-speaking neighbor to the north, the large number of

Mexicans crossing the border to work or employed by US firms in Mexico, and the millions of English-speaking tourists who visit each year, it is no surprise that there are many eager students taking English classes in Mexico's numerous language schools. What is a surprise is that so few Mexicans can speak English, considering the compulsory English classes children have to attend at primary and secondary school.

In border towns, tourist resorts, and major cities it is not too hard to find somebody with some command of English, but this is less likely in rural areas and even rarer in indigenous communities where Spanish is a second language.

One advantage of this interest in English for the visitor is that many people will want to practice their English-language skills on you, and will hopefully reciprocate by teaching you a few words or phrases in Spanish.

THE CYCLE OF FAMILY LIFE

For both rich and poor the cycle of family life—a celebration of national and religious holidays, births, baptisms, weddings, birthdays, and *quinceañera* parties—brings family and friends together. If you spend any time traveling in Mexico, or have a job working alongside Mexicans, you might be lucky enough to get an invitation to one of these events. It is certainly worth attending if you want a real insight into Mexico and Mexican life.

Milestones Marked by the Catholic Church

El bautizo (baptism), when a child receives his or her Christian name, is usually celebrated shortly after birth at a church service attended by family and close friends. This a joyous occasion where gifts are given, and there is typically a post-baptism party with music, food, and drink.

Primera Comunión (First Communion) is when young Catholics between the ages of seven and twelve first take the consecrated wafer and wine that symbolize the body and blood of Christ. Typically celebrated in a group, boys and girls dress all in white, with white gloves and a white candle symbolizing purity. Boys often wear long-sleeved *guayabera* shirts and girls wear veils or floral headbands.

Confirmación (Confirmation) takes place at around fifteen or sixteen years old, when young adults confirm their Catholic faith in the church at a special mass.

Sweet Fifteen

A major event for young Mexican girls is the *Fiesta de Quince Años* (Fifteenth Birthday Party), which is seen as a rite of passage into womanhood. The elaborate celebrations are more like a wedding than a Sweet Sixteen party in the US. Depending on the budget, the fifteen-year-old girl, the *quinceañera*, dresses up in a ball gown with a crown or tiara and is attended by her closest friends in formal suits and dresses. Traditionally, a *quince* starts with Mass in church; then there are photographs on the church steps; and afterwards there's the party. The *quinceañera* dances a waltz with her father, followed by a toast, perhaps a serenade by a mariachi band, and then a live band or DJ will play into the night. *Quinceañera* presents can be extravagant. At one time a trip to the US was all the rage for the daughters of the rich; nowadays presents can include tours around Europe, and even a car. For poorer families the dress might be homemade, and the party held at home, but everybody tries to make the day special for the *quinceañera*.

Weddings

There are few festive occasions in Mexico as joyous, colorful, or costly as a wedding. By law you are not married until you have had a civil wedding, so couples who want to marry in a church will have a civil wedding first. The easiest and cheapest option is to get married at a *registro civil* (register office), but if you can afford it a Justice of the Peace will come and marry you at home, in a historic *hacienda*, or on the beach.

In an attempt to break down taboos and promote greater tolerance for same-sex marriage the local government in Mexico City has organized several mass weddings in the central square, the Zocalo, for both heterosexual and LGBT couples.

For foreigners wanting to marry other foreigners in Mexico, the requirements are quite straightforward and Cancun and Cozumel have become popular destinations for beach weddings, especially among Canadians.

Foreigners wanting to marry Mexicans in Mexico must apply for a special permit known as a *Permiso para Contraer Matrimonio con un Nacional* in the federal state in which they plan to tie the knot .

Traditional Church weddings in Mexico can be lavish affairs, like something out of a *telenovela*. Traditions include the *lasso*, or wedding cord, which is a rosary symbolizing eternal unity placed in a figure of eight around the couple or their wrists, and the *arras,* thirteen gold or silver coins given by the groom to the bride. Mayan weddings can include a blessing by a shaman with copal incense.

Wedding receptions are lively, with mariachi bands, tequila, and traditional food. One colorful tradition is the *baile de billete*, in which guests pin bills to the bride and groom as they dance around the room. Another tradition is *el muertito* ("the little corpse"), where the band plays the funeral march to signify that the groom's days of partying are over, and he is thrown up into the air by the male guests. In Veracruz, a Huastec tradition is to serve guests a huge stuffed *tamale* called a *zacahuil*.

chapter six

TIME OUT

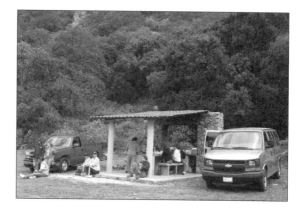

The Mexicans enjoy their leisure hours as they do their fiestas: with family and friends, and preferably with food, drinks, and music. Although they work hard—with long office hours and even longer hours for rural workers—they also play hard. The annual calendar of folk festivals and public holidays offers plenty of opportunities for carousing, and on weekends people gather in groups at local parks to play sports, enjoy a picnic, or just laugh off their troubles and down a few *chelitas* (beers). The more adventurous head off to the country's many beaches, archaeological sites, or *pueblos magicos* (picturesque towns) to soak up the atmosphere, chow down on local specialties, and share quality time with loved ones. Museums and cultural institutions are also popular weekend destinations, especially in the big cities.

However the Mexicans relax, food plays a part. Despite the arrival of US fast-food chains, they are natural foodies at heart, and eating out still revolves around a devotion to authentic Mexican flavors and ancient recipes. People are fiercely proud of their culinary and musical traditions, which have been recognized by UNESCO as unique cultural expressions that must be preserved for future generations.

A vibrant arts scene includes internationally praised painters and poets, a hugely diverse music scene, world class museums and galleries, colorful folk arts, and a film industry that continues to produce award-winning movies and launch the careers of actors, directors, and cinematographers.

Football is king when it comes to spectator sports, followed by baseball and boxing. But Mexicans also have homegrown sports such as *charreria* (rodeo), the country's official national sport, and *lucha libre* (freestyle wrestling), with larger-than-life *luchadores* donning masks, capes, and tights to delight their baying fans.

MEXICAN FOOD

For a real taste of Mexico you need only follow the crowds to a bustling street market where the dining experience is as gastronomically rewarding—and as potentially challenging to the taste buds—as at the fancy new restaurants where Mexico's top chefs are reinventing old favorites in new ways. The variety of dishes and ingredients on offer is truly overwhelming, and you would need years to try all of the country's regional dishes.

Many people arrive with a misconception of Mexican food based on the Tex-Mex concoctions popular in the USA and Europe, such as *burritos* (wheat tortilla wraps) or hard-shell tacos stuffed with shredded meat, refried beans, guacamole, and thick cream. It also comes as a surprise to many to hear that *chilli con carne* is not Mexico's national dish—it's not!

Most dishes start with a *tortilla*, a circular flat bread usually made from corn dough, although wheat *tortillas* are popular in northern Mexico. Served piping hot from the griddle, *tortillas* are used to mop up food in place of a fork or spoon.

The First Fusion Food

Mexican cuisine has been called the first fusion food, born from the collision of New World and Old World ingredients and the novel combinations that ensued. Some 8,000 years before Hernán Cortés arrived in Veracruz in 1519, the Pre-Hispanic inhabitants of present-day Mexico were eating a diet based on the cultivation of corn, beans, and squash, sometimes referred to as the "three sisters" because they grow so well together and complement each other nutritionally.

Corn was considered a sacred food by the Aztecs and the Mayans. It was the staff of life, ground to a paste on a *metate* (a rough stone grinding slab) to make the dough for *tortillas,* cooked on a *comal* (clay griddle), and *tamales,* balls of corn dough stuffed with other ingredients and steamed in a corn husk or banana leaf.

The Aztecs harvested *nopales* (cactus paddles) and *tunas* (prickly pears), and they fermented the sap of the maguey or agave plant to make a mildly alcoholic drink called *pulque.* In Lake Texcoco they harvested green algae called *tecuitlatl* (spirulina), which they formed into cakes and ate like cheese. Meat came from *guajolote* (turkey), *pato* (duck), *venado* (deer), and *conejo* (rabbit), but played only a small part in a diet in which most of the protein came from beans, or insects such as *chapulines* (grasshoppers), *chinicuiles* (maguey worms), *escamoles* (ant eggs), and *ahuatle* (water-fly eggs). Pre-Hispanic people also ate *huitlacoche* (or *cuitlacoche),* a fungus that grows on corn, and *jícama,* a thick, crunchy root vegetable.

Many ingredients that we take for granted today first came to Europe from Mexico, such as tomatoes, avocados, chilies, pineapples, vanilla, and cacao, which the Aztecs made into a foamy chocolate drink with chilies. Into Mexico the Spanish brought spices from the East, citrus fruit, sugarcane, apples, grapes, onions, garlic, rice, wheat, milk, cheese, chicken, pork, lamb, beef, and herbs, such as coriander.

The resulting Mexican cuisine is a unique, complex, and sophisticated culinary tradition, which in 2010 was declared by UNESCO as an Intangible Cultural Heritage of Humanity.

Little Cravings

Antojitos ("little cravings") are essentially snacks, the sort of finger food served up at *tianguis* (street markets) and small restaurants. The ultimate *antojito* is a *taco*— simply a small *tortilla* with a meat or vegetarian filling or topping. Tacos have been called "the most democratic of Mexican foods" because everybody, from the lowliest laborers to the richest mega-moguls, eats them.

Popular fillings at *taquerias* (taco stands) include *carnitas* (marinated pork), *campechano* (beef and chorizo sausage), *chicharrón* (pork rinds), *arrachera* (skirt steak), *picadillo* (ground beef), *birria* (goat), *guisado* (chicken or beef stew), *cabeza de res* (the meat from a boiled cow head), *rajas* (roasted *poblano* peppers cut into strips), *nopales* (thin slices of cactus paddle) and *huitlacoche* (Mexican truffle).

In Baja California and on the Pacific coast they make *tacos* with fish and seafood. In Oaxaca you can try them with *escamoles* (ant eggs). Popular in Mexico City are *Tacos al Pastor,* a variation on the Middle Eastern *shawarma* brought to Mexico by Lebanese immigrants. Marinated pork is skewered on a metal spike to form a *trompo* and cooked as it rotates. The meat is shaved off and served with a slice of pineapple from the top of the *trompo*.

What makes *antojitos* so addictive are the fresh dressings and zingy *salsas* (sauces) you pile on top. Typical accompaniments are a squeeze of lime or lemon, *cebolla* (chopped onions), *cilantro* (coriander), *pico de gallo* (chopped tomato and onion, literally "chicken beak"), *guacamole* (mashed avocado), *salsa verde* (green sauce made from *tomatillo* and chilies), *salsa roja* (red sauce made from fresh tomatoes and chilies), *salsa de chipotle* (a smoky sauce made with *chipotle* peppers), and fiery chilies like *habaneros* and *jalapeños* for those daring enough to try.

Fresh From the Sea

Mexico has nearly 6,000 miles (9.6 km) of coastline, and the waters of the Pacific, the Gulf, and the Caribbean provide an abundance of *pescado* (fish), including *atún* (tuna), *huachinango* (red snapper), *jurel* (jackfish), and *mero* (grouper). At the beach, fish is usually grilled whole or in fillets, with salt, lemon, and garlic, and served with rice, avocado slices, and *ensalada de col* (cabbage slaw). *Mariscos* (shellfish) include

A GLOSSARY OF STREET FOOD

Elote: Corn on the cob cooked on the grill, smothered with butter or mayo, rolled in chili powder and cheese, and served on a stick.

Esquites: Shucked corn cooked up in a pot with mild chillies and salt, served in a cup with crumbly cheese and a squeeze of lime.
Flautas: *Tortillas* rolled into flutes and deep-fried. **Enchiladas** are similar but must be bathed in a salsa. **Enfrijoladas** are bathed in a creamy bean sauce.
Huaraches: Thick, oval tortillas in the shape of a *huarache* (sandal), covered with beans, cheese, and a meat or mushroom topping.
Quesadillas: Folded tortillas filled with string cheese, mushroom, chorizo, and potato, or *chapulines* (grasshoppers).
Sopes: Small, circular corn dough shells, filled with refried beans, cheese, and a meat or vegetable filling, and topped with fresh chopped tomato or lettuce.
Tamales: Corn dough stuffed with pork, chicken, *salsa verde,* or *mole*, steamed or boiled in a corn

husk. In Oaxaca, Chiapas, and the Yucatán they wrap *tamales* in a banana leaf.

Tlacayos: Oval *tortillas* usually made from blue corn, stuffed with beans, and topped with cheese, onions, *nopales*, or *requesón* (*ricotta*).

Tlayudas: Baked *tortillas* topped with refried beans, shredded beef, Oaxacan cheese, and other ingredients. Also known as "Mexican pizza."

Tosta: A bun cut in half and stuffed to bursting with meat, or any other ingredient. In Jalisco, a *tosta ahogado* (drowned) is drenched in a spicy red salsa.

Tostadas: Fried *tortillas* topped with refried beans and any of the usual *taco* toppings.

camarones (shrimp), *pulpo* (octopus), *calamares* (squid), *langosta* (lobster), *cangrejos* (crab), *callos* (scallops), and *ostiones* (oysters).

The freshest seafood is to be found at beach resorts, but most big towns and cities in the interior will have a *marisquería* (seafood restaurant) or *coctelería* (serving seafood cocktails like *ceviche*). Mexico City, Monterrey, and Guadalajara have some very high-end restaurants serving sophisticated seafood dishes.

Seafood is particularly popular during Quaresma (Lent) and Semana Santa (Easter), when Catholics refrain from eating meat. On Christmas Eve it is traditional to eat *bacalao* (salt cod) with a sauce of tomatoes, olives, chilies, and capers.

The signature dish of Veracruz is *huachinango a la veracruzan*—red snapper cooked in a tomato sauce

with olives and *jalapeños*. Another Veracruz specialty, considered a surefire hangover cure and powerful aphrodisiac, is *Vuelve a la Vida* ("return to life"), a *caldo* (broth) of squid, octopus, crab, and whatever else is in season. In some places it is served as a seafood cocktail, made *ceviche*-style with lime, onion and chilies.

Mexican *ceviches* differ slightly from the Peruvian versions, as the fish or seafood is usually diced and served on a *tostada* (fried tortilla) with slices of avocado.

REGIONAL DISHES

Chiles en nogada: Cooked up in 1821 by nuns in Puebla to honor independence hero General Augustín de Iturbide, this delicious Independence Day dish patriotically combines the colors of the Mexican flag. Green *poblano* chilies stuffed with *picadillo* (ground beef) are bathed in a white sauce made from *nueces de nogal* (walnuts) and sprinkled with red pomegranate seeds.

Mole: Pronounced *moh-lay*, this ground mixture of chilies, nuts, and dark chocolate is used to make a thick sauce that is poured over chicken or turkey. *Mole Poblano*, from Puebla, is considered Mexico's national dish, but Oaxaca has seven *mole* recipes of its own, combining local herbs like *hoja santa* with almonds, dried fruits, nuts, and chili varieties like *arbol*, *ancho*, *pasillo*, and *guajillo*. *Manchamantel* ("tablecloth stainer") is a *mole* made with pineapple and spicy *chorizo*.

Cochinita Pibil: Pork rubbed with *achiote* (annatto paste), marinated in orange juice, wrapped in banana leaves, and cooked in a *pib* (Mayan earth oven). This is the signature dish of the Yucatán, where *recados* (sauces) feature bitter orange for a sweet and sour flavor.

Posole (pozole):
A stew of hominy
and pork with a
garnish of chopped
cabbage, radish,
and avocado slices
from the states of
Sinaloa, Michoacán,
Guerrero, Zacatecas, Jalisco, Morelos, and CDMX.
White *posole* is made without chilies, green *posole*
is flavored with *tomatillo*, and red *posole* gets its
kick from red chilies.

Vegetarians and Vegans

There are plenty of fresh fruits and vegetables to be
found in Mexico. At food stalls in markets you can
easily put together an order of traditional *tacos*,
gorditas, *quesadillas*, or simple corn tortillas with cheese,

bean, or *nopal*
(cactus paddle)
toppings. These
are easily turned
into mini-meals
with the addition
of the fresh
garnishes that
accompany
most dishes.

It is also possible to find vegetarian and vegan
restaurants in the big cities, at chic resorts that cater
to an international crowd, and at some beach hostels
catering to backpackers. However, there is no
widespread understanding in Mexico of what it actually
means to be a vegetarian, and you should always take

care when ordering food. Asking if a dish is *sin carne* only means "without red meat," not "without meat." Bear in mind that vegetable soups are often made with meat stock, beans are often cooked with chunks of pork, and many dishes are fried in *manteca* (pork lard). When a friend explained to a waiter in Guadalajara *"Soy vegano"* (I'm a vegan), the response was a bemused *"Eso es como un martiano?"* (Is that like a Martian?).

Desserts

Traditional desserts include *flan* (crème caramel), *pastel de tres leches* (three-milk cake), and *pastel de elote* (corn cake). Fruits cooked in *almibar* (syrup) like *ciricote* (geiger fruit) are often served with cheese to offset the sweetness, and

tropical fruit combos of mango, papaya, and guava are also popular desserts.

Delicious ice creams, called *nieves* ("snows"), range from creamy concoctions of chocolate, coconut, and condensed milk to fruit sorbets. *Raspados* are snow cones made on the street from shaved ice and flavored syrups. *Paletas* are homemade popsicles.

DRINKS

Juices made with water, sugar, and ice are called *aguas frescas* (fresh waters). Flavors include *tamarindo* (tamarind), *piña* (pineapple), *jamaica* (hibiscus flowers), *betabel* (beetroot), and *horchata* (rice and cinnamon). If you're concerned that unfiltered water was used in the preparation of *aguas frescas* in street markets, opt for freshly squeezed *jugos* (juices). *Licuados* are shakes made with milk, ice and sugar. *Refrescos* (soft drinks) include all the usual US sodas as well as local brands like Jarritos and Mundet with flavors like *guayaba* (guava) and *manzana* (apple).

For a java kick to get you started, good-quality coffee is widely available, but it's also worth trying *café*

de olla ("pot coffee"), a combination of coffee, cinnamon, and sugar traditionally prepared in a clay pot. Herbal teas like *manzanilla* (chamomile) are readily available, but English-style teas are harder to find. For a flavor of the Pre-Hispanic past try *atole*, a hot, creamy, cornmeal drink sweetened with *piloncillo* (raw sugar). *Champurrado* is *atole* with chocolate.

Alcohol

While tequila and *mezcal* (mescal) are Mexico's most famous spirits (see page 107), the country also produces a large selection of good quality beers. *Cerveza* is the Spanish word for beer, but you're more likely to hear Mexicans ordering *una chela* or *una fría*. "*Vamos a echarnos unas chelitas*" is a slang way of saying, "Let's have some beers."

A TAXING SOLUTION TO SUGARY SODAS

Despite the country's rich culinary traditions, enviable variety of exotic fruit juices, and markets overflowing with fresh produce, Mexicans are among the highest *per capita* consumers of *refrescos* (soft drinks) in the world, particularly US sodas like Coca Cola. Combined with an unhealthy diet of *comida chatarra* (junk food), this has led to an obesity epidemic and a spike in related health conditions such as diabetes.

In 2014, the Mexican government moved to tackle obesity by implementing a 10 percent tax on sugar-sweetened beverages. Initial studies showed a 12 percent fall in sales of sodas in the first year the tax was applied, but only time will tell if it will help to reverse Mexico's slide into obesity.

Two brewing giants dominate the local market. Grupo Modelo, which is owned by the Belgian brewing giant Anheuser-Busch InBev, makes Corona, Negra Modelo, Modelo Especial, León, Victoria, and Pacifico. Its rival Cervecería Cuauhtémoc Moctezuma is a subsidiary of Dutch brewer Heineken and makes Sol, Dos Equis, Tecate, Indio, Bohemia, Carta Blanca, and Superior. The bigger bottles of beer on sale have their own names: a *caguama* ("turtle") or *ballena* ("whale") is any bottle containing 900 ml to a liter. The larger *caguamón or ballenón* contains 1.2 liters.

Cheladas and *micheladas* are lime juice shandies spiced up with worcestershire sauce, tomato juice, or clamato (clam broth and tomato juice). They are typically served in an ice-cold pint glass with salt and chili around the rim, or sticky sweet and sour sauces like chamoy. *Pulque*, a creamy, viscous "beer" made from the fermented juice of the *Agave* (or maguey) plant, was a sacred drink in Aztec times and until the 1950s the preferred drink of the poor, the working classes, and bohemians. Nowadays, beer rules supreme and it's much harder to find *pulquerías* (*pulque* bars), where *blanco* (straight *pulque*) is sold alongside colorful *curados* (*pulque* flavored with fruit juices, coconut, and wheat). In Mexico City historic *pulquerías* have become hangouts for students and hipsters (see page 110). In Tlaxcala State there are *Ruta del Pulque* tours to visit historic *haciendas*, see how the *aguamiel* (juice) is extracted from the plant, and try a few jars of the finished product.

Mexico may not be famous for its wines, but some award-winning reds and whites are grown in northern Baja California. The first grapes were planted here by Jesuit and Franciscan missionaries in the 1700s and thrived in the Mediterranean-like climate. Places like Valle de Guadalupe and Valle de Santo Tomás are now a mecca for wine lovers who come to try the local chardonnays, nebbiolos, and sauvignons and tour the vineyards of top bodegas such as Monte Xanic. In August a major wine festival coincides with the *vendimia,* the annual grape harvest. Aguascalientes, Coahuila, Durango, Queretaro, Sonora, and Zacatecas also produce wines. but 90 percent of Mexican wine is produced in Baja California.

TEQUILA OR MESCAL?

Mexico's most famous export must be tequila, a party-starting spirit known the world over for the "tequila slammer," a drinking ritual involving salt, lemon, and a shot glass. Mexico's other famous liquor is mescal (*mezcal*).

Technically, tequila is a mescal. To earn its name it has to be made solely from the blue agave (*Agave tequilana*) and can only be produced in the states of Jalisco, Tamaulipas, Michoacan, Guanajuato, and Nayarit. Mescal, meanwhile, is made in Oaxaca, Durango, Guanajuato, Guerrero, San Luis Potosí, Tamaulipas, Zacatecas, and Michoacan from up to thirty varieties of agave. *Espadin* is the predominant species in Oaxaca, where most mescal is still produced on *palenques* (small farms) using traditional methods.

The best tequilas and mescals are made from "100 percent agave", meaning no other sugars were added during the distillation process. *Plata* (silver) is unaged tequila and is the best mixer for cocktails such as Margaritas. *Oro* (gold) gets its golden hue from a colorant and should not be confused with the superior quality *Reposado* (rested), which has spent from two months to a year in oak barrels. *Añejo* (aged) is usually smoother, with subtler flavors, and has spent at least a year in oak barrels. *Extra Añejo* has spent at least three years in oak.

Real connoisseurs are increasingly seeking out single-estate mescals from small, family-run *palenques* where combinations of agave species and artisanal production methods create highly prized variations on the smoky, earthy tones of this 600-year-old spirit. Note that *aficionados* of tequila and mescal don't slam; they sip.

EATING OUT

Rich or poor, Mexicans love to eat out. Starting with breakfast from taco stalls or juice vendors, eaten on the run, and continuing with lunch from a *fonda* (small eatery) serving *comidas corridas* (set lunches), there is a vast variety of snacks available on the streets, and a huge range of restaurants serving food and drinks into the early hours.

Some visitors may be surprised, given the quality of Mexican cuisine, to find so many fast-food chains from north of the border in Mexico's cities and towns. Step into a shiny shopping mall, and the food court will be dominated by US-style restaurants or homegrown copies. However, head over to recognized restaurant districts and you'll find all types of cuisine, from Italian pizzas and pastas to high-end gourmet cuisine served in sophisticated surroundings.

At weekends the local love of food extends to village squares and parks, as families and friends gather to relax with picnics and barbecues.

TIPPING

Mexico has a tipping culture, and many people rely on a *propina* (tip) to supplement a meager income. Some depend on them for their livelihood. Everybody who helps you out in some way will appreciate a few pesos in return, from bellboys and maids, to waiters, toilet attendants, and the boys who help pack your groceries at the supermarket.

Some cafés and restaurants add a *propina* (tip) to the bill, but generally it is up to the customer to leave 10–15 percent extra for the waiting staff, and more if service is exceptional. At food stalls on the street or in markets there is no obligation to tip.

For hotel staff, calculate tips of around US $1 and upward. Tour guides may be on very low salaries, especially indigenous guides in remote areas, and the equivalent of a few dollars will be much appreciated. There is no need to tip taxi drivers.

If a group of mariachi musicians start serenading you at a bar, and you appreciate the song, you can give them the equivalent of a few dollars, but don't feel obliged to pay for music if you didn't ask them to play. They'll soon move on to the next table.

NIGHTLIFE

You can get a drink at pretty much any time of the day or night in a Mexican *cantina, taverna,* or bar. Some places will even serve customers a free *botana* (savory snack) after a certain number of drinks. There was a time when it was frowned upon for women to swing through the cowboy-style doors into a *cantina*, and you can still see old signs on some traditional establishments refusing entry to women, minors, and uniformed soldiers.

More fun are the countless bars and pubs that spill on to the streets of most towns and cities, where you can sit at a table and watch the world go by. *Pulquerías* (bars serving *pulque*) used to be plentiful back in the days when the painter Frida Kahlo and her Bohemian buddies used to hang out in them. Today, they are worth seeking out to experience firsthand a truly pre-Hispanic Mexican beverage. Decorated in Aztec-style murals, Las Duelistas in Mexico City is a veritable shrine to *pulque* and attracts a young hipster crowd that has helped to make *pulquerías* trendy again.

Mexicans love to dance, and there are countless bars and clubs in cities and towns that have live music or DJs playing traditional Mexican music, *cumbia*, *salsa*, rock, pop, or the latest chart hits. Tourist resorts in Baja California, Acapulco, and Cancún have a year-round party scene that is particularly wild during Spring Break.

Wherever you are in Mexico, be aware that bars with flashing neon lights in out-of-the way places may be *casas de citas* (brothels).

MUSIC

Mariachi music is the soundtrack to Mexican life—the music of the serenade, the bullfight, the rodeo, the backing for the birthday song "Las Mañanitas," the highlight of a *Quinceañera* party or a wedding, and the sad accompaniment for the jilted lover drinking alone. Originating in Jalisco State, mariachi is rooted in the *charro* (cowboy) traditions of the central highlands and northern border states, but has become a national expression of *mexicanidad* (Mexicanness).

But there is much more to Mexican music than mariachi. The popular tune "La Cucaracha" is a *corrida,* Ritchie Valens' rock and roll hit "La Bamba" is an adaptation of a *son jarocho* from Veracruz, and in the Huasteca region the *son huasteco* features trios playing violin, *huapangera* guitar, and the small, five-string *jarana* guitar.

Veracruz and the Yucatán have a historical connection to Cuba, and there is a strong musical tradition of *boleros* and *trova* sung by artists like the Afro-Mexican singer Toña la Negra, Los Panchos, and Armando Manzanero. In the far north the musical tradition of *corridas,* polkas from Germany, and accordion music has spawned several genres from the oom-pah-pah of *norteño* groups such as Los Tigres del Norte to the brass-heavy *cumbias,* the romantic *boleros,* and the brash *narco-corridos* of artists like Los Tucanes de Tijuana or El Komander, who have both penned songs in honor of Joaquín "Chapo" Guzmán, glorifying the gangster lifestyle of the *narcos.* An alternative version of *norteño* by electronic collective Nortec has had considerable success in Latin America and the US.

MEXICO CITY'S MARIACHI MECCA

Salon Tenampa in Mexico City's Plaza Garibaldi is a shrine to the greats of mariachi music, or *rancheras*. The bar was opened in 1925 by Juan Hernández, who was already bringing musicians from his hometown of Guadalajara to play in the capital before the mariachi boom took off in the movies in the 1940s. The walls of the Tenampa are decorated with huge paintings of mariachi greats like Pedro Infante, Jorge Negrete, José Alfredo Jiménez, Vicente Fernández, and more modern interpreters of the genre like Alejandro Fernández and the flamboyant Juan Gabriel, the Liberace of Mexican music. Among the famous women gracing the walls are Amalia Mendoza, Lola Beltrán, and the gravel-voiced Chavela Vargas.

Customers pay about US $10 to request a song from a group of mariachis in the bar, and as the tequilas flow and the night wears on the impassioned singing and cowboy yelps grow ever louder. The classic line-up includes singer, violins, trumpets, classical guitar, *vihuela* (five-string guitar), and *guitarrón* (a large bass). Outside in the plaza, troupes of musicians dressed in sombreros and silver-studded *charro* (Mexican cowboy) outfits serenade passers-by or wait to be whisked off to weddings and parties.

Mariachi favorite "Cielito Lindo" (Pretty Little Heaven), with its catchy "Ay, ay, ay" chorus, has become an unofficial anthem for Mexicans all over the world.

In recognition of mariachi music to the culture and identity of Mexico it was included by UNESCO on its Intangible Cultural Heritage list in 2011.

Rock music faced state repression in the late 1960s and early '70s, as it was linked to student protests. Influential rock bands include El Tri, Caifanes, and Maná, known as the U2 of Mexican pop rock. The big bands of the late '90s were indie group Café Tacuba and Molotov, who combined political lyrics with punk, rap, and metal to create a sound that is still widely influential today.

Contemporary artists include Julieta Venegas, Camilo Lara, who explored electronica with the Mexican Institute of Sound, and Mexrrissey, a band that cover Morrissey songs in Spanish. Lila Downs has reinvented traditional folk songs and mariachi classics for a new generation.

CULTURAL ACTIVITIES

Mexico is a cultural melting pot that includes everything from the very traditional to the very modern. On the same day you might find yourself enjoying Aztec dance, a wild folk festival, and the rigorous disciplines of ballet or contemporary dance. Artworks range from the pre-Columbian ceramics of ancient civilizations to the sacred carvings of gilded colonial churches, the revolutionary murals of the 1930s, and the conceptual conceits of modern galleries.

Mexico City has more museums and cultural institutions than any other city in the world, and the streets are filled with buskers and street theater to complement the concerts and plays performed at the city's many cultural venues.

Much emphasis is placed on the work of the Mexican artist Diego Rivera. Some of his most important historical murals, depicting the rich history of Mexico, can be seen on the walls of Mexico City's National Palace. Rivera is also renowned for his tumultuous on-off love affair with Frida Kahlo, Mexico's most famous artist, and their lives and work can be enjoyed on a visit to the homes where they lived, which have been opened to the public. Frida Kahlo's Casa Azul (Blue House) is always swamped by visitors seeking insights into her highly personal art, but head down to Diego Rivera's personal collection of pre-Columbian art, the Museo Anahuacalli, and you will have the place to yourself.

The Mexican muralists David Siqueiros and José Clemente Orozco also deserve attention, as does abstract painter Rufino Tamayo, who has a museum dedicated to his work in Mexico City.

CINEMA

During the Golden Era of Mexican cinema in the 1940s and '50s hundreds of movies were made in Mexico launching the careers of comedians like Cantinflas and Tin Tan, singers like Pedro Infante, and *divas* like Dolores del Rio. During those years Spanish director Luis Buñuel came to live and work in Mexico, producing award-wining arthouse movies like *Viridiana* and *The Exterminating Angel*, and Mexico City became the film capital of Latin America. The 1970s and '80s saw a decline and a reliance on "*sexicomedias*" and low-budget indie films to keep the industry alive as TV took over from cinema and Hollywood movies reigned at the box office.

A renaissance known as El Nuevo Cine Mexicano (new Mexican cinema) came in the 1990s with critically acclaimed movies such as *Como Agua Para Chocolate* (*Like Water for Chocolate*) directed by Alfono Arau. In the twenty-first century the violent but poetic *Amores Perros* (*Love's a Bitch*) directed by Alejandro González Iñarritu, and *Y Tu Mamá También* by Alfonso Cuarón were huge international hits. Huge success in Hollywood has followed, with Alfonso Cuarón winning an Oscar for Best Director in 2014, and González Iñarritu winning for *Birdman* and *The Revenant* in 2014 and '15. Meanwhile, director Guillermo del Toro has gone from the Spanish fantasy movie *Pan's Labyrinth* to mainstream Hollywood with *Hell Boy*. Mexican cinema continues to thrive on the indie cinema circuit and at the big city multiplexes, which also offer all the usual US movies (with subtitles).

MEXICO IN THE MOVIES

For a quick snapshot of Mexican society, watch the movies that have captured the national imagination in recent years. In *Nosotros Los Nobles* (*The Noble Family*), Director Gaz Alazraki shines a scornful light on the nation's pampered rich kids, the *mirreyes;* it is a comedy about a billionaire businessman who decides to fool his three children into believing he has lost every penny so that they can learn the value of hard work. Released in 2013, it is Mexico's biggest grossing movie.

Another comedy, *Ley de Herodes* (*Herod's Law*) delivers a devastating expose of the corruption that kept the Partido Revolucionario Institucional, PRI, in power for seventy years. Luis Estrada's 1999 movie is a must-see for anybody interested in the politics of power.

Carmín Tropical is a modern film noir set in the fishing village of Juchitán, in Oaxaca. Rigoberto Perezcano's movie delves into the little-known world of *muxes,* men from Zapotec communities who dress as women and have been treated as a third gender since pre-Hispanic times.

Como Agua Para Chocolate (*Like Water for Chocolate*) is the 1992 award-winning movie by Alfonso Arau of Laura Esquivel's magical realist novel of family recipes and repressed passion set against the backdrop of the Mexican Revolution.

El Infierno (*Hell*) is a black comedy by Luis Estrada, made in 2010, that follows a migrant deported from the USA who returns home only to get sucked into the seedy and violent world of the narco "El Cochiloco" (the Crazy Pig). It exposes the futility of the drug war and the chaos and corruption that drug trafficking bring in its wake.

SPORTS

The pre-Columbian civilizations of Mexico played a ritualized ball game linked to human sacrifice that is described in the *Popol Vuh*, a Mayan creation myth. Nowadays, when it comes to passion, pride, and personal sacrifice, the king of sports is *fútbol* (soccer).

Other popular sports are baseball and boxing. One of the greatest Mexican boxers of all time is Julio César Chávez, who won six world titles in the featherweight, lightweight, and light welterweight divisions over a twenty-five-year career, including thirteen years in which he was undefeated in eighty-seven bouts.

Football (Soccer)

It was Cornish silver miners who brought their love of savory pasties and addiction to soccer to Real del Monte in Hidalgo State in the mid-nineteenth century. By 1900 the British miners had set up the first *fútbol* club in nearby Pachuca, and *pastes* (Cornish pasties with a chili kick) were firmly established as a favorite local dish. Pachuca is still one of Mexico's top teams, playing in the Liga MX against Guadalajara, Toluca, and Club América, based at Mexico City's enormous Estadio Azteca.

Every weekend thousands of people in stadiums across the country cheer on their local teams; millions more tune in to local and international soccer matches at home, while many others will head out to a bar to watch a match with friends. When they're not watching soccer, people are playing it, in five-a-side leagues, or in a kick-around in the park. Everything stops when the national side El Tri (El Tricolor) is playing. It has won the CONCACAF (North America, Central America, and the Caribbean) Gold Cup seven times since 1991 and qualified for fifteen World Cups, making it to the quarter-final in 1970 and 1986 (the years Mexico hosted the tournament). Fans are used to the highs and lows of the beautiful game, but Chile's crushing 7–0 defeat of Mexico in the 2016 Copa America was dubbed a national humiliation.

In the country that brought the world the Mexican Wave, the atmosphere in stadiums is festive and family-friendly. However, the roar of *"Eeeeeehhh! Puto"* every time the opposition goalkeeper takes a goal kick has not been well received abroad, earning the national side reprimands and fines from football's governing body, FIFA. Fans argue that chanting *"Puto"* (male prostitute) has nothing to do with homophobia but is simply a long-held tradition.

Charreria

Combining culture, tradition, costume, revolutionary history, horse riding, mariachi music, and *mezcal*, is it any wonder that *charreria* (rodeo) is the official national sport of Mexico? The *charro* (cowboy) with his broad-brimmed sombrero, short jacket, and spurs is seen as quintessentially Mexican, an image reinforced by actors from the Golden Age of Mexican cinema like Pedro Infante and Jorge Negrete, strong, silent types who sang sad *rancheras* (mariachi songs) when they weren't riding the range. The *charro*

tradition is also a part of Mexico's revolutionary history and is linked to icons like Emiliano Zapata. Every September the best rodeo riders come to Guadalajara to compete in *charreadas* (tests of horsemanship) at the Mexican National Charro Championship, although there is as much art as sport involved in the roping and bull-riding competitions.

Lucha Libre

With their masks, capes, and tights, Mexico's *luchadores* look more like comic-book superheroes than professional wrestlers, but anybody who attends a bout in Mexico City's Arena Coliseo or Arena Mexico will quickly see that the blood, sweat, and tears are real. *Lucha Libre* (freestyle wrestling) evolved from Greco-Roman wrestling in the nineteenth century, but the masks and elaborate aerial maneuvers that make it such an exhilarating spectacle were adopted in the 1930s and '40s. The most famous Mexican wrestler is El Santo, a huge celebrity in the 1950s who appeared in cartoon strips and a series of movies where he saved the world from aliens and werewolves. He was even buried in his trademark silver mask.

Contests focus as much on entertainment as on sport, pitting *tecnicos* (heroes) against *rudos* (villains) in battles of good against evil. *Luchadoras* (female wrestlers) have their own league, and bouts are as frenetic and bruising as the men's. Wrestlers known as *exoticos* are flamboyant gender-benders. *Cassandro*, the first openly gay *luchador*, is an *exotico*

who has done much to challenge macho attitudes to homosexuality in the ring and in society as a whole.

Others who have used *lucha libre* to lead social protests are Super Barrio, who led a campaign in the late 1980s to highlight the plight of slum dwellers, and Fray Tormenta (Friar Storm), a parish priest who kept his orphanage afloat with the proceeds from his bouts. The Hollywood movie Nacho Libre is loosely based on the exploits of Fray Tormenta.

Bullfighting

Bloodthirsty and brutal as it may be, and despite growing calls for it to be banned, bullfighting is alive and well in Mexico. The Plaza México in Mexico City is the largest bullring in the world, with some 41,000 seats, although nowadays it hosts more pop concerts than *corridas* (bullfighting tournaments). The late-October-to-May bullfighting season coincides with the recess in Spain, allowing big name *toreadores* (bullfighters) to fight in Mexico. The highlights of the Feria de San Marcos in Aguascalientes are bullfights and cockfights, and the bull ring in Tijuana, Baja California, attracts tourists from the US who come to experience the cultural and ritualistic elements of the *corrida*. Animal rights campaigners have called for a nationwide ban on bullfighting, following statewide bans in Sonora in 2013, Coahuila in 2014, and Guerrero in 2015. Polls show that the majority of Mexicans would support such a move.

SHOPPING

You can find all the usual shops in Mexico's mega-malls, but for a real appreciation of the enormous range of food, shoes, clothing, household goods, toys, spiritual paraphernalia, pets, and *piñatas* on sale you have to explore the country's covered markets and *tianguis,* the street markets that pop up on specific days.

Mexico City has hundreds of local markets specializing in different goods, including the Mercado de San Juan near the center, where chefs go to buy exotic meats like crocodile and wild boar, and the Mercado de Sonora, famous for its potions, spells, and *brujos* (witches).

Handicrafts

There are loads of good *artesanías* (handicrafts) to pick up in Mexico—a legacy of the country's sophisticated pre-Columbian past, the large number of surviving indigenous groups, and the abundance of folk artists putting a new spin on traditional designs.

Mexican mines have produced high-quality silver for thousands of years, and the mining towns of Taxco, Zacatecas, and San Luis Potosí are home to skilled silversmiths who produce fine jewelry in pre-Columbian and modern designs. Buy from shops rather than on the street, and look out for the 925 sterling silver mark.

The papier-mâché skulls, skeletons, and masks made in Pátzcuaro, Oaxaca, and CDMX for the Día de los Muertos (Day of the Dead) celebrations are creatively creepy. Reproductions of famous Day of the Dead prints by the engraver José Guadalupe Posada are readily available, and every year brings new variations on characters like the Calavera Catrina (Skeleton Catrina).

The symbolic and highly psychedelic folk art of the Huichol, from the Sierra Madre Occidental, is rooted in ancient myths and shamanistic visions brought on by the hallucinogenic peyote cactus. The highest artistic expression of the Huichol spirit world is expressed in elaborate yarn paintings, but commercial handicrafts featuring the same symbolic designs are sold in Puerto Vallarta, Guadalajara, and San Miguel de Allende.

TRAVEL, HEALTH, & SAFETY

Before you travel, make sure you have adequate travel and health insurance to cover you for treatment in case of accident or illness. It pays to read the small print and find out what is and isn't covered, especially if you intend to engage in adventure sports such as zip-lining across Copper Canyon, caving in San Cristobal de las Casas, or swimming with whale sharks in Cancún. Before engaging in any activities like horse riding, whitewater rafting, or scuba diving, ensure that the companies offering the service are adequately covered.

The best policies available in the US, Canada, and the UK will cover you for emergency medical transport, evacuation, and repatriation. This is particularly useful if you plan to travel to rural areas, where medical services are limited and you may need to be airlifted out.

Mexico has a good transportation infrastructure that includes well-maintained highways and toll roads; modern, air-conditioned buses traveling the main routes; and busy airports serving the major cities and tourist resorts. It may be smaller than its huge neighbors to the north, but Mexico is still one of the largest countries in Latin America and is best experienced through well-planned visits to specific destinations. Traveling around is generally cheaper than in the USA or Europe, whether you go by air, bus, or taxi. With online booking available for most flights,

buses, and accommodation, it is easy to organize
your trip, unless you plan to head out into the wilds.

FLYING

There are some sixty passenger airports in Mexico,
with the main hub at Benito Juárez International
Airport serving Mexico City, and busy international
airports in Cancún, Guadalajara, Monterrey, Tijuana,
Los Cabos, Puerto Vallarta, and Mérida, and many
smaller airports serving internal flights.

The country's main carrier is Aeroméxico, the
national flag carrier that was once state-owned but
is now part of the SkyTeam alliance with Delta, Air
France, and Korean Air. A host of US and European
carriers compete for passengers to Mexico, and it
pays to shop around.

For internal flights, new, low-cost airlines are
challenging Aeroméxico Connect's dominance,
including VivaAerobus and Volaris, which is now
flying from Guadalajara to Texas. An internal flight

can cost three or four times more than a long-distance bus fare but will save considerable time. Book in advance for the best deals and try to avoid travel during the Christmas, Easter, and summer vacations, when prices are higher and there is less availability.

BUSES

The cheapest option for both long and short distance travel in Mexico is to take a bus. Hollywood often peddles the tired stereotype of poor peasants and their livestock crammed into clapped-out contraptions belching clouds of smoke as they wheeze lazily down dusty rural roads or race perilously round hairpin bends. Look hard enough in the remoter corners of Mexico and you might even come across one of these "chicken buses," as travelers have dubbed them. If you do have to take one, relax and enjoy the experience, as this kind of encounter with rural Mexican life is becoming rare.

The reality is that most major cities in Mexico have modern, air-conditioned bus stations with food fairs and free Wi-Fi where you can catch comfortable, modern, air-conditioned buses with onboard entertainment that depart frequently, are competitively priced, and can get you just about anywhere.

Mexico City has four bus terminals serving the north, south, east, and west of the country. In most cities and towns the central bus station, called the "Central Camionera," or "Terminal de Autobuses," will be on the outskirts.

There are three classes of long-distance bus—called a *camion* in Mexico, rather than an *autobus*. Top of the range and the most expensive are the executive services billed as *Primera Plus*, *De Lujo*, *Pullman*, or *Ejecutivo*. The luxury extras include hot drinks, onboard toilets, and more comfortable seats than buses in the *Primera* category, which also offer reserved seats, videos, and air-con. Lastly, *Segunda* can vary in quality, may not have air-con, and will generally make more stops along the way. Direct buses will be identified as *directo* or *expreso*.

The bigger bus companies, such as ADO, TAP, and others have good Web sites where you can book online, and have timetables showing departure (*salida*) and arrival *(llegada)* times. If you can't book online, try to get a ticket at the terminal the day before you travel, especially at peak times.

When deciding whether to take a bus or fly, bear in mind that distances can be huge. The bus journey from Tijuana to Cancún, for example, takes the best part of three days.

TRAINS

Passenger train services ceased to operate in most of Mexico following the privatization of the railroads in the late 1990s. The few surviving rail experiences include the Chihuahua–Pacific Railway, which travels through the Barranca del Cobre (Copper Canyon), considered one of the world's great train journeys. Less awe-inspiring, but stimulating in its own way, is the train that runs from Guadalajara through blue agave plantations to the José Cuervo tequila *hacienda* and distillery in Tequila, the town that gave its name to Mexico's most famous export.

RIDE THE RAILS ON EL CHEPE

With thirty-seven bridges and eighty-six tunnels, the 405-mile Ferrocarril Chihuahua–Pacífico represents a major feat of nineteenth-century engineering and is one of the last narrow-gauge railroads in North America. Known affectionately as "El Chepe," Mexico's last true passenger train offers an epic way to ride on this railroad through the Barranca del Cobre, or Copper Canyon, a truly jaw-dropping, awe-inspiring series of roughly-cut valleys that are not only deeper than Arizona's Grand Canyon but cover a wider area.

El Chepe chugs along between Los Mochis on the Pacific coast and up through the Sierra Tarahumara to Chihuahua. Passengers can choose to stop at Creel, a base for hiking, and Divisadero, where you can try local dishes and handicrafts made by the Tarahumara, an indigenous group native to the Sierra Madre famous for their long-distance running.

DRIVING

You wouldn't want to drive in Mexico City, where the peak hour norms are gridlock, car fumes, and revved up "Chilangos," as the locals are known. Whether you call it DF, or CDMX, sprawling Mexico City is just too huge to negotiate for a novice. Also, with taxi rides so affordable and the Metro system so easy to use, why bother?

Elsewhere in Mexico, when touring colonial towns, or the archaeological ruins of the Yucatán, driving yourself makes sense. In general, if you do your homework, know where you are going, have a good map or reliable app, and don't drive at night or pass through any hot spots (see page 137), driving in Mexico is no different from driving at home. What you will find is that signposting is less than adequate, toll roads are worth the money, and it pays to give other drivers plenty of leeway. Always heed local advice before setting out, and err on the side of caution.

The Roads

Outside the cities, the country's road network is very good between the main cities, and better in the north of the country than the south.

Super carreteras, or "superhighways," are the widest, at four lanes, and the fastest. They have the least traffic and the highest tolls.

Cuotas, "tolls," are the next step down, and are cheaper to use. They range in quality and width, from four lanes to one, and you are likely to encounter more trucks and buses. Always have cash handy if taking toll roads.

Libres, or "free roads," carry the bulk of the traffic and are invariably more congested. They also run through the center of towns, and some are in bad condition, but if you are not in a hurry they can give you a better flavor of the country than a toll road.

Distances are measured in kilometers and speed limits are 110 kmph (68 mph) on superhighways and toll roads, and 40 kmph (25 mph) in built-up areas, while many single-lane rural roads are restricted to 70 kmph (45 mph).

Fuel

Until recently all gas stations were run by Pemex, and fuel prices were the same across the country except along the US border, where prices are closer to US prices. It is hoped that new filling stations and greater competition will improve the service for motorists. Gasoline is unleaded in Mexico, with Magna, a *regular* 87-octane fuel and Premium UBA, 91 octane. Diesel is also available.

In rural areas and on some highways gas stations can be far apart, so fill up where you can.

Rules of the Road

Mexicans drive on the right; seatbelts are compulsory; and it is illegal to drink and drive. Foreign drivers should acquaint themselves with road signs in Spanish and keep an eye open for speed bumps (*topes*), potholes, and wandering livestock.

The Policia Federal de Caminos, or Federal Traffic Police, can offer assistance if you break down on the highway, while in towns you can approach the Policia de Tránsito for help. Mexicans are generally wary of traffic police, who, when they stop drivers, have a reputation for coming up with infractions that require the payment of a fine (*una multa*). Be polite at all times and emphasize the fact you are a foreigner. If you do get a fine, you are unlikely to get a receipt for it. If you're not happy about the service you get from the police, wait until you are safely at your destination before pursuing a complaint (*una denuncia*).

URBAN TRANSPORTATION

In Mexico's towns and cities there are several ways to get around, from local buses (*camiones*) to barely regulated minivans and microbuses known as *combis*, *micros*, and *colectivos*. Some are so that small you get to touch knees with the other passengers. For Mexico City's rapid transport system, Metrobús, you pay by prepaid smartcard, but on most buses, including *combis*, *micros*, and *colectivos* (also known as *peseros* as the fare used to be one *peso*), you pay the driver when boarding or disembarking, and they will stop when asked. In Mexico City, *peseros* have been called loud, crowded, and dangerous to ride due to their blaring music and the risk of being robbed.

Outside peak times, the best way to get around Mexico City is on the Metro, the second-largest subway system in North America after New York, with twelve lines and 195 stations.

Taxis are another cheap way to get around, and new app-cab services like Uber and Cabify offer low-fare rides compared to Mexico City's official pink and white cab fleet. To avoid problems, always take official cabs, preferably from a taxi rank, known as a *sitio,* or call a reliable taxi service and ask to be picked up.

PINK LADIES

In 2000 the Metro in Mexico City introduced special areas on platforms and carriages reserved for women and children under twelve to reduce incidents of harassment at peak hours. The local government then added pink buses for women and children in 2008, and women-friendly taxis with female drivers, which were first trialed in the town of Puebla. Many women have welcomed a respite from the ogling and flirting common on public transport, but others argue that the situation will not improve until deeply entrenched macho attitudes are tackled.

WHERE TO STAY

Visitors can find almost every kind of accommodation in Mexico, from luxury resorts catering to Hollywood A-listers to hammocks strung up in a fisherman's shack for backpackers on a budget.

Hotels are graded from one to five stars, while the most luxurious are categorized as *Gran Turismo*. Historic *haciendas*, mansions, and convents have their own category, and sometimes have limits on what they can offer due to preservation concerns, but give a real taste of Mexico's rich past. Hammocks and rustic beach *cabanas* have no stars at all, and camping is free on some beaches; but always enquire with locals first, as campers are a target for robbery in some places. Always ask to see rooms before agreeing to stay, to avoid disappointment.

Local hotel chains include Presidente Intercontinental and Camino Real, and tend to have more character than the international chains such as Marriott, Sheraton, and Westin.

HEALTH

Mexico has good-quality health care and well-equipped modern hospitals offering all major treatments for those with the money to afford them. Public health care provided by the state can be less reliable.

Mexicans often head to the pharmacy as a first port of call for minor ailments. Many medicines that require a prescription in other countries, including antibiotics, can be bought over the counter, and pharmacists can give advice. Prices are generally higher than in the US and roughly equivalent to those in the UK. If you fall seriously ill, ask for the number of an English-speaking doctor from your hotel or consulate, or ask local people for the best hospital.

Health Precautions

There are no compulsory vaccinations for visitors to Mexico. However, if you are arriving from a country where yellow fever is present, a vaccination certificate is required. Vaccinations against Hepatitis A and B, typhoid, diphtheria, polio, and tetanus (or a booster shot) are all recommended if you are traveling to remote rural or jungle areas.

ZIKA VIRUS

Carried by two species of *Aedes* mosquitoes (*aegypti* and *albopictus*), the Zika virus originated in Africa and rapidly spread through the Americas after the first cases were detected in Brazil in 2015. Only one in five people infected is thought to develop symptoms, which can include a rash, headache, mild fever, conjunctivitis, and joint pain. In Brazil, cases of Zika have been linked to microcephaly (a condition causing small heads in babies) and pregnant women have been warned to avoid areas where Zika cases have been confirmed.

In Mexico, the government has responded with a mosquito fumigation program in affected areas and the Tourism Board has produced a detailed map of where cases have been documented to allay fears and show that major cities and most tourist areas are mostly unaffected for now (check latest updates before travel). There is no vaccine for Zika. Travelers should wear long sleeves and trousers, regularly apply repellent, and sleep under mosquito nets to avoid bites from infected mosquitoes.

Malaria is present in the rural south of Mexico and up-country Yucatán, so precautions should be taken for visits to these areas.

The tropical sun is fierce, especially at altitude and even on cloudy days, so apply sunscreen and wear a hat. Mosquitoes come out to bite as the sun sets, so bring shirts with long sleeves and long pants, and slap on the bug repellent before they get you.

Pack a small medical kit with antiseptic cream, insect repellent, anti-diarrhea pills, rehydration salts, and plasters in case of small cuts or blisters.

Bring any prescribed medication with you, along with such items as contact lens solutions and/or a spare pair of glasses.

NATURAL HAZARDS

Altitude sickness: Symptoms include dizziness, headaches, and labored breathing. Regular stops and a gradual ascent will help you acclimatize. If symptoms persist, descend until you feel better.

Scorpions: In remote areas, or when camping in the jungle or on beaches, follow local advice and shake out your shoes before putting them on to avoid scorpion (*alacran*) stings. If stung by a pale yellow scorpion (*Alacran güero*, from the *Centruroides* family), seek medical attention. Always try to catch and keep the scorpion for identification.

Coral: It is easy to graze against coral when snorkeling or diving, and cuts can quickly become infected if not washed out thoroughly with an antibacterial solution, vinegar, or even your own urine. Jellyfish stings will also respond to the same treatment.

Spiders: Hairy tarantulas are the villains of many a Hollywood movie, but their bite is only slightly more painful than a bee sting. The spiders to watch out for in Mexico are the black widow (from the genus *Latrodectus*), and the brown recluse, or fiddleback (*Loxosceles reclusa*), both of which can cause serious complications, although bites are rare and anti-venom is available.

SAFETY

Mexico usually appears in the news only when there's a major drug bust or narco arrest, but despite this negative image abroad the actions of violent criminal gangs and cartels are focused on specific hotspots that can be avoided (see page 137).

As in all major cities and popular tourist destinations, there are pickpockets, opportunists, and scam artists who prey on unwary visitors, but taking sensible precautions will reduce the risk of falling victim to crime. Carjacking and highway robbery are a problem in the north of Mexico, in Sinaloa, and on remote roads in Chiapas; you should heed local warnings and avoid driving at night. A variety of strategies are employed to get cars and buses to stop, from placing obstacles in the road to posing as drivers who have broken down and need assistance. Most carjacking victims are released unharmed after their valuables have been stolen.

EXPRESS KIDNAPPING

There has been a rise in recent years of so-called "express kidnappings" (*secuestro express*), in which taxi passengers are held up at knife- or gunpoint by one or more assailants, robbed of their valuables, taken to ATMs or banks and forced to empty their accounts over a short period of time before being released.

Avoid being a target by traveling in a group with others, taking money out of ATMs inside a bank or shopping mall during the day, and calling a taxi service, or having your hotel call one, rather than hailing one in the street. If you are involved in an express kidnapping, it is best to give your assailants what they want without a fight.

TIPS ON STAYING SAFE

- Travel with others. You are safer in a group, and solo travelers, especially women, can be targeted.
- Don't attract the attention of thieves.
- Leave your gold chains, diamond rings, and expensive watches at home, and keep digital cameras and cell phones out of sight.
- Don't use ATMs in the street or at night. Try to use ATMs inside banks during the day.
- Learn some Spanish. The more you can speak and understand, the better.
- Listen to the locals. Heed advice on places to avoid, don't enter poor areas of cities and towns. Avoid danger hot spots (see above).
- Know where you are going. Don't wander around with a map looking lost.
- Don't take taxis on the street at night. Have your hotel call you a taxi, or ask them for the number of a reliable company. Or book one via Uber.
- Avoid crowds. Don't travel on the Metro in Mexico City or browse the stalls of crowded markets with anything you don't want to lose, because pickpockets, including minors, will take advantage of the crush to relieve you of your valuables.
- Use the hotel safe. Don't walk around with all your cash, but always have something on you that you can hand over if mugged.
- Carry a "mugger's wallet." This is a decoy wallet with a few small bills to make minor purchases with; an expired credit card; and an old library or gym card for authenticity.
- Have a backup. Keep emergency bills hidden in

your belt, shoes, or clothing, just in case of need.

- Let it go. If you do get held up by an armed assailant, hand over your stuff. Keep calm and do not resist.
- Copy documents. Scan your passport, airline ticket, and other documents, and email yourself and your family a copy, along with relevant bank and credit card company numbers to phone and cancel cards in case of theft or loss.

HOT SPOTS TO AVOID

While most of Mexico's major tourist centers are generally safe, the states of Guerrero, Michoacan, Morelos, Sinaloa, Sonora, Tamaulipas, and Zacatecas have all been flagged up as areas to avoid due to incidents of kidnapping, extortion, homicides, people trafficking, or confrontations between the Mexican security forces and the cartels. The once popular beach resort of Acapulco in Guerrero has been the scene of a spate of murders in recent years and travel there is not advised until the security situation improves. Travel on buses at night in many areas of the country is also not advised because of hold-ups. Before traveling consult the US State Department's latest Travel Advisory for Mexico, which gives specific advice for each state.

BUSINESS BRIEFING

THE BUSINESS LANDSCAPE

Since signing up to NAFTA in 1994, Mexico has benefited from a prolonged period of relative economic stability and growth. Sectors that have been opened up to foreign investment over the last twenty years include the automotive industry, transportation, banking, telecommunications, and, more recently, real estate, energy, and the oil industry. The result is a very diversified and sophisticated economy that is less reliant on oil revenue than it was in the past, but is still closely tied to the economic fortunes of its huge neighbor to the north.

US influence is apparent everywhere, from the two thousand Walmart outlets that dot the country under a variety of names, to the ubiquitous franchised food outlets like Starbucks, KFC, and Subway. Even Taco Bell is having a crack at selling a US interpretation of Mexico's most iconic food back to the mother country.

In the industrialized north, along the US border, the *maquiladoras* churn out some three million vehicles every year for US firms such as Ford, General Motors, and Chrysler, as well as European and Japanese car makers such as BMW and Nissan.

In banking the whole panorama has changed, with US banking giant CitiGroup which owns Banamex, now vying for customers with HSBC, Canada's Scotiabank, and the Spanish group BBVA, which took over Bancomer. The entry of these foreign banking giants has led to longer banking hours, easier online banking, and a greater range of credit options.

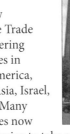

Mexico is now signed up to Free Trade Agreements covering forty-six countries in Europe, Latin America, the Caribbean, Asia, Israel, and Australasia. Many foreign companies now operate out of Mexico to take advantage of free trade access to the US market under the terms of NAFTA. In 2016, some 80 percent of Mexico's exports ended up in the USA, for example.

While low wages and a skilled workforce attract the US industrial giants to the north of the country, an increasing middle class with disposable income in the big cities is driving a growing service industry that generates some 60 percent of the country's GDP.

DOING BUSINESS WITH MEXICANS

For several years the Mexican government has been actively courting foreign investment to offset low oil prices and increase diversification, but the panorama is not all rosy. Security costs can be higher for operating in some parts of Mexico, and there are still problems with the rule of law and corruption. In short, setting up a business in Mexico takes time. You can't just fire off a few emails and jet in to shake hands and sign a contract. Organizing meetings, finding the people you need, and dealing with unforeseen delays can be a frustrating process at times. Expect your patience and flexibility to be tested.

As elsewhere in Latin America, who you know is as important as what you have to sell, and putting the time into networking and face-to-face contact will be crucial to the success of any business venture you embark upon.

Contact the business attaché in your country's consulate in Mexico for help. They will usually have an up-to-date list of local firms offering legal advice, who can produce and translate contracts. Local chambers of commerce can also be useful (see below). The key is to find people who can get you a meeting with decision makers or other important people in an organization, or get things moving if they stall.

The World Bank's "Ease of Doing Business Index" for 2016 ranked Mexico at 38 out of 189 countries. It was the highest-ranked country in the Latin American and Caribbean region and ten places above Chile, although well below the USA (7), and the UK (6). While it scored lower on "Enforcing Contracts", ranked at 41, it was again the highest-scoring country in Latin America.

Personal Relationships

Every country has its own style of doing business, and Mexico—although strongly influenced by the US management models taught at business schools—is a place where people still like to spend time on the social niceties before getting down to brass tacks.

In the past a small elite of rich families controlled the country. If you wanted to meet the decision makers and get deals done all you needed were the right friends, or an impressive last name to signify you came from *buena gente* (good people). That concept continues to a certain extent today, and initial meetings will often ignore the business at hand and revolve around chitchat about your family, your home town, and your impressions of Mexico.

Building personal relationships with potential business partners is time consuming and can be frustrating to US or European entrepreneurs who are eager to get things moving. However, trying to rush negotiations could be perceived negatively, so it's important to slow down and factor in more time for more meetings. The key is to meet people who can provide you with good recommendations and get you direct access to company chiefs and decision makers whom you would have difficulty meeting yourself. Very often you will need several visits before you see any results. Making a good impression, networking, spending time to get to know the right people, and keeping contacts fresh are important for doing business in Mexico.

Dress Code

Despite the tropical heat in many parts of the country, the dress code in Mexico is formal at meetings and business-related social events. Mexicans set great store by what you wear, and men will typically wear dark business suits and ties at top-level meetings. Although it is not considered appropriate to wear a tie without a jacket or to remove your jacket once seated, it's fine to follow what your hosts do. For women, the same corporate uniform applies as in the US or Europe, and dresses, skirts, and trousers are all appropriate attire.

Treat breakfast and lunch meetings as formal unless told otherwise, and dress appropriately for evening events or dinner, depending on the venue.

WELCOME TO SLIMLANDIA

A self-made billionaire, Carlos Slim (born 1940), the son of Lebanese immigrants, was ranked by Forbes Magazine as the richest man in the world from 2010–13, pushing Bill Gates and Warren Buffet off the top spot. His Grupo Carso conglomerate and other business concerns include such a diverse portfolio of companies—including banking, insurance, construction, real estate, media, retail, the Sanborns chain of restaurants, and Sears outlets—that some Mexican humorists have joked that the country should be renamed Slimlandia.

The tycoon also has significant investments abroad, with a sizable stake in Saks Fifth Avenue and a significant share of the *New York Times*, after he bailed the paper out with a US $250 million loan in 2009. His wealth increased significantly after the telecommunications industry was privatized in the 1990s and he acquired the state telecoms giant Telmex, eventually incorporating it into América Móvil, which also operates Telcel, Mexico's largest cell phone provider.

One Mexican investor described Slim as Rockefeller, Carnegie, and J. P. Morgan all rolled into one, and Forbes estimated his net worth at US $53.9 billion in May 2016. In Mexico City his power and influence can be seen in the shiny modern shopping malls of the Nuevo Polanco district, where the Museo Soumaya, an art museum named after his late wife, opened in 2011 to house a personal art collection of 66,000 pieces, including a hundred sculptures by Auguste Rodin.

WOMEN IN BUSINESS

Although things are slowly changing, most top managers or CEOs in Mexico are men, and macho attitudes persist at all levels in the workplace, especially in industries like construction. Women are still employed for their looks, especially in marketing and sales roles, and casual sexism persists. This attitude was expressed in 2013 by the boss of TV Azteca boss when he said women "are doing badly because they want to do everything," and suggesting they would be better off at home, raising children and feeding their husbands. Women also get lower salaries than their male counterparts and are over-represented in the informal sector—running street stalls or food outlets— where they can work with their children alongside them.

However, the number of women employed at middle-management level has grown significantly over the last five years; women are increasingly overtaking their male counterparts in the number of higher degrees gained, and female entrepreneurs are making their mark in a wide range of industries.

As a foreign woman doing business in Mexico you are unlikely to encounter any problems but you may find some of the attitudes towards women old-fashioned, even quaint, and some of the comments you receive may border on flirtatious. The key is to keep things professional, friendly, and polite.

When meeting a Mexican woman in a business environment for the first time, a warm handshake is the best approach. At subsequent meetings, and as the relationship develops, a kiss on the cheek is typical among Mexicans.

SETTING UP A MEETING

When dealing with government bodies the process of making appointments is formal and bureaucratic, and can be very slow. It's best to start at your local Mexican embassy, unless you have a direct contact, and begin with a formal letter and email in Spanish. If you can get the trade attaché at your embassy to help you with contacts things will move faster. Mexican agents or partners are even better, as they will be able to get you into the office where you can arrange a meeting in person.

With large businesses used to dealing with foreign companies a direct email in Spanish is acceptable for proposing dates for a meeting, but it should be followed up by a phone call about two weeks before the meeting and another the day before, just to check that everything is on schedule. This might seem like overkill to foreign entrepreneurs, but in Mexico, where things can change quite quickly and where businesspeople are juggling many things at the same time, you need to keep in touch, gently remind people you're coming, and use the opportunity to build a rapport.

Entrepreneurs who have spent months sending out e-mails from their home country without any concrete leads will find that once in Mexico they will start to see results. Mexicans prefer to deal with people face to face, and once they know you personally will be more likely to introduce you to other business acquaintances and help to set up meetings.

If you want fast results you will have to come to Mexico and meet people in person. Part of the challenge here, as in most places, is understanding who has the power to do business with you and sign off on deals, and how you can get hold of them.

Timing of Meetings
An important consideration when scheduling appointments is that Mexicans take their weekends and public holidays seriously and there is little chance of getting anything done on a Friday afternoon or during

the long holiday periods around Christmas and New Year, Carnival, or Easter.

The best time for a meeting is in the morning. Depending on the size of the company, you may be invited to a breakfast meeting with several executives and decision makers where you can discuss things over coffee and a pastry. These often act as pre-meetings and a chance to find out more about you. Don't be frustrated if you don't get down to business straight away. This is not the place to get a decision. The same holds true for lunch meetings.

Be aware that an invitation to dinner is probably down to hospitality and the thought of your staying in alone in a hotel in an unknown city rather than a burning desire to do business with you there and then. The key thing is to remain professional at all times, even when out on the town, and that the etiquette in Mexico is for the person issuing the invitation to pay the bill. Never offer to pay just your share of the bill; this would come across as mean. Offer to pay it all, but don't insist too much if refused, as this may cause offense. It's better to let your host pay and for you to issue the next invitation.

Punctuality

The perception persists of Mexico as the land of *mañana* (tomorrow), and in a sense it is deserved. The vagaries of traffic, and a laid-back attitude to timekeeping by some Mexicans, especially in the smaller towns, can result in a late start when it comes to meetings. A foreign businessperson, however, should always arrive on time, although not before, and will need to factor in potential transport delays when making plans. If you have to wait, even for an hour or so, or even reschedule a meeting for another day (*mañana*), this is nothing personal—just a local peculiarity that you will have to get used to. The important thing is not to get ruffled or show undue annoyance by last-minute changes and to make sure you leave room in your schedule for contingencies.

MEETINGS AND PRESENTATIONS

The formalities of a meeting usually begin with a greeting to the group of "*Buenos días*" or "*Buenas tardes*," depending on the time of day. You will be presented to each person in the room. It is typical to shake hands. (For forms of address, see pages 149 and 154.)

Bring business cards written in English on one side and the other in Spanish. Any material or brochures you bring with you should also be translated into Spanish, preferably by a local translator to get the tone right and avoid words with different meanings in different Spanish-speaking countries.

You will also need an interpreter or intermediary/ partner who can translate, even if some people in the room speak English. Generally, senior executives in large private companies speak English, but you can't guarantee it, and junior executives with key expertise pertaining to any deal may have no English at all. When dealing with government agencies you should always bring an interpreter and have a document drawn up in Spanish with the main points of your proposal.

Presentations should also be given in Spanish, preferably with an interpreter who can convey all the subtleties of your pitch if your Spanish is not up to it.

Don't be put off if there is

conversation during your presentation, or if people take phone calls or leave the room while you are speaking; this is just another example of a more relaxed attitude to doing business.

Questions may be asked in a very direct way, but don't take this as confrontational, and give calm, measured responses. The key here is to keep your cool and remain friendly and professional at all times.

NEGOTIATIONS

Having given your pitch and answered questions, don't expect an immediate answer as usually several more meetings will be needed before a deal is finalized. Very often you will be told that somebody else has to be consulted, and when dealing with government agencies that is probably the case, but in private firms this could also be a polite way of saying, "We'll think about it and get back to you."

If negotiations drag on too long, however, it probably means that the Mexican business is avoiding a straight "No," in favor of subtle hints. Having local contacts more used to the subtleties of Mexican negotiations will help to interpret the responses you receive.

CONTRACTS AND LEGAL CONSIDERATIONS

Unlike the legal systems in the US and the UK, which rely on a "common-law" system of judicial precedents, Mexico has a "written code" or "civil law" legal system like the ones in France and Spain.

Mexico's laws are a combination of its national constitution, legal codes, laws laid down in federal, state, and municipal entities, and presidential decrees. With such a complicated and wide-ranging legal landscape it is advisable to seek guidance from a well-respected law firm on all the legal issues pertaining to any potential business venture before going ahead.

Use a local lawyer and professional translator to draft contracts in Spanish and English and clarify any contractual issues before signing.

It's important to contact your embassy or business chamber for the latest updates on the legal status of foreign firms in Mexico, and issues of purchasing real estate along the coast and border areas, tariff exceptions, and repatriation of profits.

MANAGING DISAGREEMENT

If there is disagreement over a contract or payment, the first and best option is to try to deal with it straight away. Good local legal advice is essential, as going to court over a contract breach can be a protracted and frustrating process. The Mexican legal system is slow, judicial rulings can be unpredictable, and the judiciary not always impartial to external influences. The best way to avoid disputes is to maintain frequent contact with Mexican business partners, which will help to build strong personal ties and flag up issues before disputes arise. This may mean a closer working relationship than one would foster with a US or UK business partner and more time spent on the ground.

MANAGEMENT STYLE

The old-school company hierarchy where the boss is the boss and several levels of management are layered one upon another to create a classic pyramid structure is still the norm in Mexico. Formality and the use of titles is fairly widespread. At first meetings expect to start with *Señor* (Sir) and *Usted* (the formal singular form of "you") and only switch to a less formal *tu* (informal singular form) if the person you are addressing drops the formalities.

It is typical for an engineer to be addressed as *Ingeniero*, a university graduate as *Licenciado*, and a businessman with a master's degree as "Doctor." Very often the title will be included on a business card. Foreign businesspeople will not be expected to use these terms, but they do give an insight into the pecking order in a company, and knowing them will certainly help if you are thinking of setting up a business and employing Mexicans.

A foreign businessperson managing Mexican staff will be expected to act as a boss and maintain a certain distance with staff, while exhibiting enough empathy for them to be able to express their concerns.

Mexico has strict labor laws, and foreign managers will need to be up to speed with the specific prohibitions on outsourcing and per-hour contracts as well as maternity provisions, disciplinary procedures, and how to terminate employment.

DEALING WITH RED TAPE

For the uninitiated, dealing with government entities can involve hours waiting in line or time-consuming and frustrating phone and email communication. One way to speed things up is to work with local partners, business associations, or reputable agencies who already have contacts and can cut down the time it takes to negotiate the necessary red tape. For importing or exporting goods through customs, a trusted local contact is essential, and local agents are a requirement for dealing with the government.

ORGANIZATIONS THAT CAN HELP

Foreign businesses seeking to do business in Mexico but who don't have the advantage of good local connections should start by approaching the trade representative at their country's embassy or consulate, who will be able to help with local advice and a list of reliable contacts and suggestions for business partners, agents, and legal representatives.

The US Commercial Service has offices in Mexico City, Guadalajara, and Monterrey and produces a regularly updated Country Commercial Guide aimed at assisting US companies and individuals interested in investing in Mexico with key information on the commercial landscape and investment opportunities.

The UK Trade and Investment (UKTI) offices at the British Embassy in Mexico City and in Monterrey, Guadalajara, and Tijuana can advise UK businesses that want to export to or import from Mexico.

You should also approach established business associations, which can provide up-to-date information on the business climate and the market, and steer you towards reliable local partners and reputable legal firms. In Mexico City, these include the American Chamber of Commerce of Mexico, and the British Chamber of Commerce.

ProMéxico, the Mexican body promoting trade and investment abroad, has offices attached to Mexico's embassies in the US, the UK, Canada, and thirty-two other countries. (http://www.promexico.gob.mx/).

CORRUPTION

Mexico has a challenging corruption problem, particularly in relation to the judiciary, the police, and public officials, and in areas where criminal gangs are active and extortion is widespread. The country has consistently scored badly on Transparency International's Corruption Perceptions Index, where it ranks at 95 out of 168 countries, compared to the USA, which came in at 16.

Mexicans who are tired of the corruption and impunity that blight their lives have called for greater financial transparency from public officials and corporations, and some measures have been put in place to audit the affairs of public officials accused of corrupt practices.

Foreigners doing business in Mexico should steer clear of any individual or company offering a short cut to official procedures through any form of inducement, whether financial or in kind.

GIFT GIVING

When first meeting potential clients in Mexico you are not expected to bring a gift, but bringing something typical from your country—candy, shortbread, or a bottle of wine or whiskey picked up in Duty Free, or an illustrated book of your city or country—can act as good icebreakers. Gifts and treating clients to hospitality are not illegal in Mexico, and many Mexican businesses will send hampers or small gifts to clients and customers at Christmas, or to celebrate an anniversary. However, it is best not to give expensive gifts like Rolex watches or gold pens, which could be misinterpreted as bribes. Some companies, particularly large multinationals operating in the country, do not allow staff to accept gifts for the same reason.

COMMUNICATING

LANGUAGE

There is no official language in Mexico. The Mexican constitution recognizes Spanish and sixty-eight indigenous languages as national languages, although Spanish is the language of government and is spoken as a first language by some 95 percent of the population. Even in the few areas where indigenous groups maintain their own languages as a first language, most people speak and understand Spanish.

The Spanish spoken in Mexico is known as *castellano,* from Castile in Spain, although it differs from the Spanish spoken in Madrid in several ways. First, there is no lisp on the letters *c* and *z*, so *cerveza* (beer) sounds like *sir-vay-sir*. Second, there is a singsong accent, most noticeable in central states like Jalisco—an echo of the ancient Aztec tongue Nahuatl. Then there are the many words particular to Mexico. Even a cursory glance at the map shows the prevalence of indigenous place names, and Mexican Spanish has also been enriched with many words taken from Nahuatl, Mayan, Purépecha, and other languages both living and extinct. As the Spanish conquistadors encountered creatures and foods they had no names for they added them to the language. While *aguacate* (avocado, from the Aztec *ahuacatl*), *tomate* (tomato, from *tomatl*), and *chile* (chili pepper, from *chilli*) entered the universal lexicon, many other words remained only in Mexico. So when hipsters in

Mexico City invite you to meet their *cuates* (pals) to drink some *pulque* (fermented cactus sap beer), they are using Aztec words.

Speaking Spanish

Every child educated in Mexico receives some schooling in English, and many Mexicans have spent time in the US or have family members living there. However, apart from people living on the US border, those employed in the tourist industry, and well-heeled sophisticates, most Mexicans you meet on your travels can only muster a few words or phrases along the lines of "How are you?," "What is your name?," and "Where are you from?"

The more Spanish you can learn before you go, the better. Not only will you be able to ask for things and understand the replies, but you will also find it easier to make meaningful contact with the people you meet. Any attempt you make to speak Spanish will be appreciated, from a simple greeting like "*Hola!*" to a local expression like "*Que onda, güey?*" ("What's up, dude?").

Learn a few phrases like "*Sabroso, gracias!*" ("Tasty, thanks!"), to show your appreciation of food at dinner, or "*chido*" ("cool"), which might raise a smile. If you plan to spend longer in the country there are good schools teaching Spanish to foreigners in Mexico City, Guadalajara, Monterrey, Oaxaca, Mérida, Puerta Vallarta, and expat hangouts like Puebla and San Miguel de Allende. Some schools offer homestays with a Mexican family, which is a great way to fast-track your Spanish and get a real insight into the food, culture, and daily life of the country.

Good Manners

Good manners and respect for others are very important in Mexico. When entering a shop or office people will say to those present "*Buenos días*" or "*Buenas tardes.*"

To show respect, address people as *Señor/Señora/Señorita*, and the elderly as *Don/Doña* with their first name. If you don't know the marital status of a young woman, use *Señorita* and let her correct you.

When being introduced it is customary to say "*Mucho gusto*" ("Pleased [to meet you]"), or "*Es un placer conocerle*," or simply "*Un placer*" ("It's a pleasure"), followed by your first name.

In restaurants or at dinner people say "*Buen provecho*" ("Enjoy your meal") to other diners.

SPEAK LIKE A MEXICAN

Textbook Spanish will help you get by in Mexico, but to get under the skin of the country and fit in with new friends a few typical words and phrases can go a long way. Always use slang expressions with a certain caution, and assess your audience before you use them. Not all Mexicans use the same expressions, and a word that provokes mirth in northern Mexico might cause offense in the Yucatán.

"Chilangos," as the residents of Mexico City are called, have a reputation for the liveliest street slang. For a flavor of how impenetrable Chilango can sound to the untrained ear (imagine a midwesterner trying to untangle Cockney rhyming slang), listen to Café Tacuba's version of Jaime Lopez's song "Chilanga Banda," which starts: "*Ya chole chango chilango. Que chafa chamba te chutes. No checa andas de tacuche. Y chale con la charola*." ("That's enough Mexico City monkey boy, your job is really lame, you don't look good in a uniform, even less with your official badge.")

Other Languages

The sixty-eight recognized indigenous languages in Mexico include Nahuatl, with 1.5 million speakers, Yucatec Maya, with about 750,000, and Mixtec, with 425,000. In total, out of the ten million Mexicans who identify as belonging to an indigenous group, only 6.5 million speak an indigenous language. Some languages have so few speakers that they are on the verge of extinction, although much is being done to revive indigenous cultures and customs, as speaking

Caguama	40 oz bottle of beer
Carnal	Buddy, Bro
Chela	Beer
Chido	Cool
Fresa	Snob, stuck-up, preppy
Güey	From the word *buey* (ox); it means "dude" in the expression: "*Que onda, güey*?" (What's up, dude?)
Híjole!	Wow! Whoa! Expression of surprise
Órale!	"Let's go!" Used in the Northern Mexican expression "*Órale, vato*?" (What's up, dude?)
Padre	Cool. *Padrisimo/a* (super cool)
Mande?	Perhaps the Mexican expression you will hear most; it means the equivalent of "Can I help you?"
Naco	Low-class, cheap, tasteless. Taken from Totonaco (the indigenous group), this pejorative term shows up Mexico's racial and class prejudices
No manches!	No way! You're kidding! A politer version of "*No mames!*" Often combined with *güey*

the language is one of the criteria for access to government aid programs. It is estimated that 130 distinct languages have been lost since the violent conquest of Mexico by Spain and the subsequent attempt to unify the country under one language after independence in 1821.

PERSONAL SPACE

Mexicans don't have the same strict rules on personal space that you find in some countries. They are happy to get up close, and are more hands-on when meeting. In a formal setting, men will shake hands as in the US or Europe, and you can expect a back slap or even a bear hug from friends. The etiquette between women, or between a man and a woman, is a single kiss on the right cheek. This is not a romantic kiss, just a touch of the cheeks, or an air kiss. A casual wave could be seen as standoffish.

SPEAK LIKE AN AZTEC

The Aztec Empire might have come to a bloodthirsty end with the siege of Tenochtitlán and the conquest of Mexico by the Spanish, but the language of the empire, Nahuatl, lives on in everyday speech. This is one of the features of Mexican, as a language, that sets it apart from the Spanish spoken in Spain and other Latin American countries:

Spanish	Aztec	English
Cacahuate	*Tlacucahuatl*	Peanut
Chamaco	*Camahuac*	Boy
Chapulin	*Chapulin*	Grasshopper
Chicle	*Chictli*	Gum (chewing gum)
Chile	*Chilli*	Chili pepper

BODY LANGUAGE

Mexicans are not as animated as Argentinians when speaking, but they do use their hands to illustrate a point, and it's important to understand the gestures they use. It can be considered rude or aggressive to beckon to somebody with the fingers pointing upwards, like a cop directing traffic. Mexicans do it with the palm facing downward and the fingers pointing down, like a one-handed doggy paddle.

To indicate that someone is being stingy or tightfisted it is typical to bend the arm and tap the elbow. From this you get the expression "*No seas codo*" ("Don't be elbow"), which means don't be cheap, get your wallet out.

Some gestures can be misinterpreted and should be avoided. In the US it is not uncommon to see people tapping or thumping the heart with the fist

Chocolate	*Xocoatl*	Chocolate (bitter water, in Aztec)
Coyote	*Coyotl*	Coyote
Cuate	*Cuatl*	Friend (literally, twin)
Elote	*Elo-tl*	Corn on the cob
Escuincle	*Itzcuintli*	Small child (literally, hairless pre-Colombian dog)
Guacamole	*Ahuaca-molli*	Avocado sauce
Guajolote	*Guajalote*	Turkey
Mecate	*Mecatl*	Rope
Nopal	*Nopalli*	Prickly pear (edible cactus paddle)
Ocelote	*Oceloti*	Ocelot
Tecolote	*Tecolotl*	Owl
Zopilote	*Tzopilotl*	Vulture

to show respect, as in the hip-hop gesture of "Peace, out"—but in Mexico it mean you are indicating, and not in a pleasant way, that somebody is gay.

THE MEDIA

The Mexican media scene is opening up to greater competition, but is still dominated by old giants like Televisa. The biggest media conglomerate in Latin America, Televisa is also the largest producer of *telenovelas* (soap operas) and other Spanish-language content in the world and supplies programming to TV and cable operators throughout Latin America and the US.

A less enviable record for the country is the amount of violence that journalists face. Reporters Without Borders (RSF) has described Mexico as the most dangerous country in the Western Hemisphere for journalists. More than a hundred media professionals have been murdered since the year 2000, and journalists across the country who investigate crime or corruption face daily intimidation and harassment by drug cartels or public officials who want to silence them.

Television

The two big players in Mexican TV are media giant Televisa and TV Azteca, which have two national channels each and broadcast a daily diet of news, talk, and gossip, game and reality shows, and sports, as well as US program, such as cartoons, sitcoms, and dramas, dubbed into Spanish. The government also runs two channels that focus on Mexican music, arts, and culture.

Increasingly Mexicans in the big cities are watching their TV via satellite or cable from companies like Cablevision, SkyTV, or DirecTV, which offer movie channels and a variety of English-language news, sports, and entertainment from the US, Canada, and the UK. The arrival of streaming services such as Netflix, offering instant access to the latest TV series and movies, has shaken up the local market as more Mexicans are getting their TV fix online.

Radio

Mexico also has the largest network of Spanish-language radio stations of any country in Latin America, and radio is still an important source of news for rural communities. Every kind of Mexican music can be found on these stations from *norteño* and *banda* to mariachi, *rock en español, boleros*, pop, electronica, and the latest US chart hits. Many churches and evangelical groups operate radio stations to spread their word, and indigenous groups have stations that broadcast in Maya, Nahuatl, and Mixtec.

Newspapers

Newsstands in Mexico are weighed down with all the newspapers and magazines available. Newspapers with good national and international coverage include *El Universal, El Economista, El Financiero, El Nacional*, and *El Sol de Mexico. Reforma* is considered a good newspaper for a critical analysis of events in Mexico, as is the weekly magazine *Proceso* and the left-wing daily *La Jornada*. Less serious, and certainly less sensitive, sensationalist tabloids such as *El Gráfico* feature lurid cover photos of semi-clad celebrities or shocking images of crimes or accident scenes to attract attention on newsstands. Hundreds of newspapers serve regional markets and individual towns and cities, some run by large conglomerates, others by independent editors.

English-Language Publications

More than a million US expats live in Mexico—the largest group in the world—and there is huge daily traffic between the two countries along the 1,989 miles (3,201 km) of the shared border, so it is no surprise that US publications are easy to find in the big cities, though some will be a day old, as will British papers. The *International Herald Tribune* and the *New York Times* can be picked up at newsstands or in chain restaurants such as Sanborns. Weekly international news magazines such as *Time*, *Newsweek*, *The Economist*, and a wide variety of lifestyle magazines are also available.

Based in Mexico City, *The News* is an English-language newspaper published from Monday to Friday and available at newsstands in tourist and upscale areas of the city. It can also be accessed online.

Places with large expatriate populations from the US and Canada have their own daily and weekly publications, such as the *Guadalajara Reporter* in Guadalajara and the *Ojo del Lago* ("Eye of the Lake") in the expat haven of Chapala, in Jalisco State. In San Miguel de Allende there is a weekly paper with a calendar of local events called *Atención*. Others include the *Yucatán Times* in Mérida and the *Mexico News Daily* in Puerto Vallarta.

SERVICES
Telephone

While landlines offer cheaper rates for calls, it can be a lengthy process to have one installed, especially in rural areas, so many Mexicans rely on cell phones to communicate. The most popular contract or pay-as-you-go cell services are TelCel, AT&T, and Movistar, and

competition for users has seen prices fall. To cut down on cell phone charges Mexicans are increasingly using social media apps that allow voice communication where Wi-Fi or broadband access are available.

To use a US or European phone in Mexico with a local Sim card the phone must be unlocked.

USEFUL TELEPHONE NUMBERS

Most numbers in Mexico have eight digits, combining the area code and local number.

Interstate within Mexico: 01 before the number

Operator services: 040

Country code: 52

City Codes: Guadalajara 33; Monterrey 81; Mérida 999; Cancún 998

Emergency: Police, Fire, Ambulance 911

Internet

After Brazil, Mexico has the biggest Internet market in Latin America, with 58 million users in 2016. Mexicans can access the Internet in an increasing variety of ways following the opening of the telecommunications sector in 2013. Greater competition and lower prices have driven a rapid growth in mobile access as AT&T and Movistar take on Telcel for customers, and many cable companies now offer home broadband, telephone, and TV packages. While Wi-Fi is available in many hotels, restaurants, and cafés, it is not always free. Visitors to the country will find Wi-Fi is not as widespread as in many other Latin American countries, especially in rural areas, but there is usually an Internet café where local students do their homework, play video games, or chat online. Social media is hugely popular in Mexico, with almost as many registered Facebook users as Internet users. Social media apps like Whatsapp, Twitter, and Snapchat are also popular.

Mail

Main post offices (*oficinas de correos*) are open from 8:00 a.m. to 8:00 p.m. Monday to Friday, and from 8:00 a.m. to 3:00 p.m. on Saturdays. The postal service is generally slow and unreliable, especially when sending letters or parcels abroad, or receiving them from abroad. Instead Mexicans rely on the many private local courier services or international couriers such as DHL, FedEx, and UPS. If you just want to send a postcard home there are red and yellow mailboxes in large hotels, on the streets, and at airports.

CONCLUSION

Mexico is one of those countries that people feel they know because of the oft-repeated stereotypes of Mexican people, music, and food portrayed in Hollywood movies, TV shows, and magazines. As we have tried to show, the reality is much more complex and nuanced. Mexicans don't just sit in the shade waiting for *mañana*. There is a strong middle class; people work hard to get ahead; they believe strongly in education; and have built one of the most powerful economies in Latin America.

There is *machismo*, but much is being done to improve gender equality and defend the rights of the LGBT community. There is a violent drug war being played out in the country, especially in the states along the long US border, but it's a war that rarely touches tourists and the safety tips outlined in Chapter 7 should help to minimize the risk of a negative experience.

Some stereotypes do have a grain of truth in them. The Mexican people put family first, and will happily drop everything to celebrate a folk festival with the religious zeal and Bacchanalian gusto it deserves. They love mariachi music, and it touches their soul when the trumpets begin to play and familiar songs are sung. But there is also a vibrant pop, rock, and electronica scene, and people also enjoy *cumbia*, the oom-pah-pah of *norteño,* and chart hits from north of the border.

Mexican food and drink also tick all the boxes you might imagine. You don't have to go far in Mexico to find tasty finger food that is fiery with chilis, and tequila is the tipple of choice all over the country. However, you'll also find that Mexicans don't just stick a wedge of lime in their beer—they pour it into a large glass with chili power around the rim, add the juice of squeezed limes, ice, and clam juice, and call it a *chelada* or a *michelada*. They don't slam tequila with salt and lemon—they sip it as if it were a fine brandy.

Most of the food you find in Mexico is not mouth-searingly hot. Rather, it is so diverse and unusual that you could take weeks exploring the mouth-watering offerings at just one of the maze-like covered markets in Mexico City, and still have only a slim idea of the many regional specialities that make travel around the country so gastronomically rewarding. The true magic of Mexico is that it continually serves up surprises.

We hope that, whatever your reason for visiting Mexico, whether you are a tourist or a business traveler, this book will give you the confidence to delve a little more deeply into the history and culture of this dynamic country and to discover for yourself the warmth, vibrancy, and fascination of the Mexican way of life.

Further Reading

Azuela, Mariano. *The Underdogs*. New York: Random House, 2002.

Christenson, Allen J. *Popol Vuh: The Sacred Book of the Maya*. Norman, Oklahoma: University of Oklahoma Press, 2007.

Cortés, Hernán. *Letters from Mexico*. New Haven, Connecticut: Yale University Press, 2001.

De las Casas, Bartolomé. *A Short Account of the Destruction of the Indies*. London: Penguin Classics, 1992.

Díaz, Bernal. *The True History of The Conquest of New Spain*. Indianapolis: Hackett Publishing, 2012.

Esquivel, Laura. *Like Water for Chocolate*. New York: Anchor Books, 1995.

Fuentes, Carlos. *The Death of Artemio Cruz*. New York: FSG-Macmillan, 2009.

Greene, Graham. *The Power and the Glory*. London: Penguin Books, 2003.

Grillo, Ioan. *El Narco: Inside Mexico's Criminal Insurgency*. London: Bloomsbury Press, 2012.

Harrison, John. *1591: A Journey to the End of Time*. Swansea: Parthian Books, 2015.

Herrera, Hayden. *Frida: A Biography of Frida Kahlo*. New York: Harper Perrenial, 2000.

Leon Portilla, Miguel. *The Burning Spears: The Aztec Account of the Conquest of Mexico*. Boston: Beacon Press, 2006.

Lida, David. *First Stop in the New World: Mexico City*. New York: Riverhead Books, 2009.

Lowry, Malcolm. *Under the Volcano* (first published 1947). New York: Harper Perennial, 2010.

MacDougall, Christopher. *Born to Run: A Hidden Tribe, Superathletes, and the Greatest Race the World Has Never Seen*. New York: Vintage Books, 2011.

Paz, Octavio. *The Labyrinth of Solitude, The Other Mexico, and Other Essays on Mexico*. New York: Grove Press, 1994.

Pierre, D.B.C. *Vernon God Little*. London: Faber and Faber, 2004.

Rainsford, Catriona. *Urban Circus: Travels With Mexico's Malabaristas*. London: Bradt, 2013.

Rulfo, Juan. *Pedro Páramo*. London: Serpents Tail Publishing, 2000.

—. *The Burning Plain*. Austin: University of Texas Press, 1971.

Thomas, Hugh. *The Conquest of Mexico*. London: Harvill Press, 2004.

Tree, Isabella. *Sliced Iguana: Travels in Mexico*. London: Tauris Parke Paperbacks, 2008.

Index